TWENTY YEARS ON THE CAPE

My Time as a Surfcaster

By Frank Daignault

MT PUBLICATIONS

MYSTIC, CONNECTICUT

Library of Congress Cataloging-in-Publication Data

Daignault, Frank, 1936-
    Twenty Years on the Cape

    Includes index
    1. Surf fishing — Massachusetts — Cape Cod. I. Title
II. Title: 20 years on the cape.
SH507.D35   1989   799.1'66145   89-2377

ISBN 0-929775-02-3

 MT
PUBLICATIONS

No part of this book may be reproduced in any form without permission in
writing from the publishers. Any questions, comments, etc. should be
addressed to:
                    MT PUBLICATIONS
                    Two Denison Avenue
                    Mystic, CT 06355

Parts of this have appeared in different and abbreviated form in *The Fisherman, Salt Water Sportsman,* and *Fishing World.*

Dedication

For nearly all of the 31 years that my wife, Joyce, and I have been together, sportsmen of the beaches, gun clubs, and streams of New England have reminded me of how lucky I have been to have a wife beside me to share my sport. While I appreciate that this was never intended as an admonition, it has always made me uneasy to think that anyone might believe that I did not know what I had. Moreover, in their efforts to remind me of my enviable social wealth, they could never have known how absolute the relationship remains. There is far more to a marriage than having a partner that can shoot grouse, fly cast, and haul great stripers from the high surf. A wife from such a marriage would be able to bear beautiful children, nurse him and those children in a time of need, aid in his education, share in his literary interests and grieve in his disappointments. In addition to being a lover and companion, such a person would share in the production of one's books.

Anyone lucky enough to have such a wife and who had to be reminded of that fortune, would be unworthy.

To Joyce. My God, who else.

Frank Daignault, July 1988

Contents

Contents

Forward

Springing from the idea that surfcasting isn't what it used to be, there has been a rising interest in the so-called good old days in general and in Cape Cod in particular. The Cape understandably enjoys top rank order among the best places for the practice of the surfcaster's art. That is not to say that we can overlook Montauk, Rhode Island, or the Outer Banks, because these indeed do enjoy a special place for consideration. What sets the Cape aside from the other places is that it .was last to go under the repressive regulation that society has found necessary in the management of dwindling coastal resources. Moreover, it is the place where I happened to spend the most of my life surfcasting for striped bass. We tell it, because we saw the last of the Cape's surfcasting glory days and because there is no one else who knew that good life with a greater intimacy.

One of the problems that comes up in the passing of a generation is that much of what was done then is wrong now. As you read this autobiographical account of the Daignault family, my family, you will see that there is an undeniable preoccupation with taking all the stripers one can lay his hands on and carting them off to market—the kind of thing that today would leave even a moderate conservationist wretching in the dunes. Knowing this, we dare not tamper with the ethic of the times and thus chronicle the feelings that prevailed with the full knowledge that modern surfcasters are certainly more conservation minded than we were. Indeed, the mood of the time and the inspiration that came from fishing for gold must remain intact or the very catalyst of the good life would be missing. We fished for money because we were poor; later we fished for money because we knew nothing else.

Because we sold fish, we assume no role of either being on the dark side of ethic or the law. Thus, we disassociate ourselves from the stylish scenario of having been there in some criminal capacity as has been the case with so many reformed drug addicts who lecture our children or defrocked government heroes who lectured for fat honorariums. We are not reformed because we didn't do anything wrong in the first place. At the time that all this took place bass were a commercial fish, netted in every state but Massachusetts. Bear in mind that there is no more primitive means to take fish commercially than from the beach with rod and reel. Even Biblical accounts of fishermen indicate more efficient means. And there was no striper problem during most of the years of which we write. Supported by well entrenched tradition, hauling a few bucks from the Atlantic was then an honorable endeavor.

Try, as you read, to keep the perspective of time in place. Envision a young couple in their mid-twenties with four babies, discovering the economic realities of life in our society. Ask yourself if you would take small children out into the uninhabited wasteland of a distant peninsula in a two-wheel-drive truck that has been discarded by any number of previous owners. Try to note the subtle changes in perspective that I experienced while progressing from wide eyed newcomer to dyed-in-the-wool surfcaster regular. Such movement through the chain of command comes with the years. While time is being considered, do not overlook that my hair has turned white since that first night on Long Bar with "Muff," though the night itself may have played some part. Adjust fish checks for inflation and you may

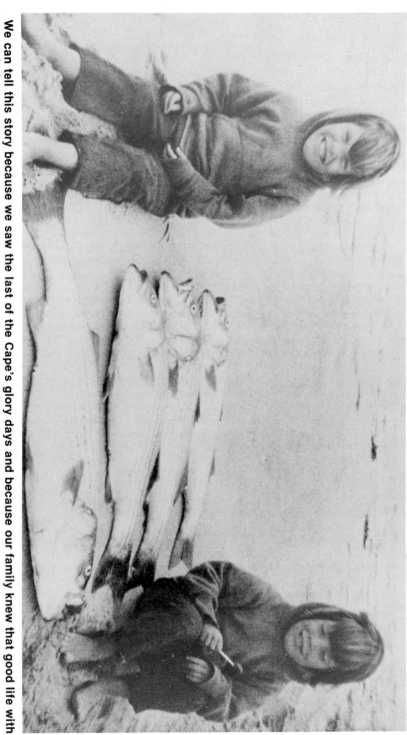

We can tell this story because we saw the last of the Cape's glory days and because our family knew that good life with a great intimacy.

recognize that there was serious folding green in store for those casting with a will. If fishing for money turns you off, that may be because of the diversity in our backgrounds as well as the subtle changes in sport fishing ethic. Indeed such change is never uncommon in the passage of time. For instance, as a younger man I sold my blood every spring to buy a new spinning reel. Later, only winos and druggies sold their blood; later still, nobody buys it.

We had a life on Cape Cod fishing the beach for striped bass. This great fish inspired an aura of adventure within us keeping us together in a common ground that gave Joyce, my high school sweetheart, and me a purpose in life with more meaning. In spite of the artificiality of such endeavors, what else in life that engages man truly enjoys meaning; one need only look at how quickly we are replaced or how rapidly our memory fades to see that all is fleeting and that the individual enjoys the least permanence of all. Thus, this self-indulgent thirst for adventure is justifiable in the face of the alternative life of engaging power feeds in an engine lathe in some smoky, steaming industrial plant — a life I left. If I hadn't, life, as I had known it and which was devouring my Joyce, might have tormented our marriage out of existence. And she, as young, beautiful, and virgin-like in every facet of her manner, having borne our first when she was only 17, would have slipped out of my very grasp.

Nothing of our lives was the product of any special wisdom. If anything, our course was plotted out of fear for the marriages around us that failed, out of the economic desperation of having too many children too soon, and, as a consequence, being able to do little else but fish the beach. By the time Joyce was 21, we had four children which proves that there is no greater oppression than that which we impose upon ourselves. Of course, those regrets have long faded. One of the many joys that children brought to our life on Cape Cod was being able to see them assimilated into the surf-casting fraternity. They would wander for miles free of fear during the day, fish the nights when the call was clear, sleep when their eyes closed; the only clock here was the tide. Theirs was a ceiling of stars and their carpet spanned horizons of sand and sea.

Off to Cape Cod.

CHAPTER 1

Nauset Beach

Summer 1988. Once they passed into the cooler water east of Monomoy, the rhythm of their pace seemed to accelerate. There were a few thousand of them, their flanks glistening slightly among the ones nearer the surface. Still, from most angles they were ghostlike because their lateral lines caused them to blend with the ever changing strata lines of the water and its bars. They moved oblivious to the currents of the Monomoy Cut, unconscious to the rise in tide from the north, determined by a course set by a millennium of previous generations. Not big striped bass by the standards of the fishermen who waited for them, but they were still the most sought gamefish of the Cape Cod surfcaster. By sunset they had covered the four miles of South Island's outside and began to feel the subtle warmth of sun heated Pleasant Bay, even taste the scent of sand eels borne by an ebbing tide.

On the north bank of the inlet a gaggle of four-wheelers huddled at the limit marker and a half dozen casters lined the sand spit that curved around the opening. A small swimming plug broke the surface, the monofilament tightened, and the surfman on the shore pumped the tip slightly before starting his retrieve. One lineside broke from the others, its proximity sense a fraction keener than that of the others, lunged at the plug then felt the steel of its hooks.

As the other casters made contact, it brought the few who were standing around to the water—all except two.

I was sitting on the tailgate with Joyce watching their excited movement to the water. And though neither of us spoke, I know that we were both thinking about what striper fishing used to be.

June 1965. Whatever the bass fishing was along Nauset Beach, it could be improved upon at the inlet. Here, during full tide, currents hurried along the outside to the opening of Pleasant Bay where they collided with the warmer water of Nantucket Sound as it swept past Monomoy Island. Some days, when the sou'west was blowing particularly hard, cresting swells would have their tops blown off and the mist would stream behind, catching the sun in hues of color before fading. East of the inlet a bar formed in an acute angle from the beach, the product, somehow, of the way the water moved to and from the inlet.

At low water the surfcasters would walk out on Long Bar, drive sand spikes into the sand, cast seaworms, and wait. Weekends the rods formed a fence like line for close to a mile. On the top their beach buggies formed a similar line.

These were former large delivery vans that might have once been used to deliver bread or milk to a thousand Mom and Pop stores around New England. While little might have been done to restore their mechanical performance, they characteristically had attractive paneling interiors, bunk beds, sinks, stoves, propane lanterns and the creature comforts needed for a family. The better ones had five speed transmissions, plenty of weight over the rear wheels, and over-size tires. Key to a vehicle's mobility were the tire pressures, which were cautiously dropped enough, according to the weight of the buggy, to put the tire in a sag that was half flat looking. All possessed more than was needed in surfrods which were carried in racks along the outside wall. For movement from one fishing spot to another, there was a line of tubes on the front bumper where a surfman could hur-

Long Bar on Nauset Beach the way we found it. Few plugged for stripers as the mode of fishing had been bottom fishing with seaworms.

riedly drop his active rods before changing locations. Fishing machines in every sense of the word, they were also homes for families, the interminable spawn of the fishermen, who splashed about in the surf by day then hid among the shadows of the trucks soon after sunset in the traditional games of children.

Long Bar and Chatham Inlet are a gathering place for serious surf-casters, because few casual fishermen are willing to endure the grueling, 11 mile torture of driving a trail that is sometimes washed out by the sea during the higher night tides or cooked in the heat of day to make an engine overheat. Indeed, the trip down the beach is a veritable obstacle course of mechanical complexities. Even if you were lucky enough to have the sou'west cool down the water in the radiator, it was a certainty that the same wind was creating an underpressure in front of trucks coming off. Even if you started with tire pressures that were low enough, the heat would expand the air inside before long making you wonder if you had read the gauge right. You could lose your nerve when the track looked too tough, back up to avoid it, then bury the buggy when the rear wheels left the track and all the kids would start crying. Once, on a Friday night after working all day, I made the same wrong turn five times in the fog until I gave up on the trails. Instead I chose to ride the high water mark of Pleasant Bay until the buggy unaccountably stalled. Examination revealed that a matted wad of seaweed had wrapped itself around our drive shaft so tight—large as an oversize beach ball—that it was dragging in the track and raising our rear wheels off of the sand. After hours of slashing away with a fishing knife thankful all the time that the clutch hadn't burned out, we were mobile again. All the time I had worked, the sand fleas had been gnawing at the exposed flesh above my belt and at my neck, raising infected welts that blistered and itched for days. Small wonder that the south end of the beach was inhabited only by dyed-in-the-wool surfcasters.

Among them was a veritable who's who of striper fishing—not famous names in a media sense because Channel 12 never cared who caught the most striped bass; not big guns as one might see them in the tournament results of sweetwater bass fishing. These were the pros of Nauset Beach, a place where those who fished were grateful that its best men were relegated to obscurity. When you fish the finest striper grounds in the world it is a whispered fact. Thankfully, there are no recorded annals of striper fishing which document the names of Charley Murat, Frank Woolner, the Felices—Eddie and Purgo, Muff Briere, Rusty Watson. Men like these went without eating to catch striped bass. They were people who were so charismatic, so special, that you exaggerated to others about your relationship with them. It was part of your manhood facade to claim brotherhood with them. Nights, during mid-watch hunts for striped bass, when you told of a great hit of fish that might have happened on a better night you colored it so that Eddie Felice was hauling back on a cow to your left, Woolner was dropping a 40 pounder into his camouflage panel truck behind you, and Murat was backing and giggling with a brute in the wash. With names like that it had to be true; for some of us it was.

It was my first year teaching, my first summer of freedom, when I met Muff Briere, a scruffy little old guy from Warwick, Rhode Island, who had the mind and body of the 28 year old that I was. To me, then in 1964, Muff was an old guy, close to 50. But he had a vitality for killing stripers, and he could spit out enough words about a woman's anatomy to make you think that his interest in either had never waned. I don't know why I liked Muff, really loved him, but if he said it, it was true somehow. Maybe deep down I

Among the regulars fishing there for many years before we arrived was Frank Woolner, Editor of *Salt Water Sportsman.*

sensed that there was something that he could teach me.

"You stick on this bar with me tonight, kid, and we'll do a job. We'll wait 'til the others is all gone. Pay for worms and gas and ice cream for the kids."

Tide slacked at sunset while a relatively flat surf rolled short foamers on the bar now exposed at low tide. Anglers were spread the full distance seemingly painted in position because there hadn't been any action. Muff seemed to know that the slow going was beginning to bother me but he periodically uttered words of encouragement. When Long Bar is exposed, it is only two inches above sea level. Thus, when the tide began to rise, water was sliding over the bar end within minutes. Once full darkness had set in, fishermen were moving off, passing us as they went, at an ever increasing number. Muffy had marked a spot where the sand was a trifle higher than the rest, a place where, he said, we would have to cross later, after all the "idiots," as he called them, were gone.

Within an hour the bar was awash and we had to load everything into our parkas. Even the sand spikes were taking water and we were backing the two rods apiece that we were using when one of Muff's went down. That was only the beginning. When I tried to help him, he motioned me back to my own rods pointing out above the roar of the rising surf that there would be more. One rod was limp, out of contact with the sinker, and I reeled up the slack to find life writhing on the end when I set. With all the water rising on the bar, I tried to think where we were going to put all these bass he had promised as I fought my first one.

"Got the rope, kid?"

Muffy was running his through the gills of an eight pounder when I came over with a like fish, the third between us. By now water was knee height but the two foot waves would hit us, sending sheets of water into our faces as he lashed the 20 foot stringer to my belt. It was too difficult to get around for spacing the rods, or even walking seaward for a cast. By the time it had been dark two hours the stringer was so loaded that it tugged viciously at my waist every time a foamer broke beside us. I couldn't keep two rods baited, having long since abandoned one, using it to mark the spike of the rod I fished. When I was sure the active stick had been cleaned off, I left it and baited the spare. Once, while trying to shift them, I had difficulty getting the butt into the top of the spike until I realized that I couldn't control it because a bass was hauling it down. And though I fought to hold my place against a now pulling tide, several times I felt the dropoff behind with one foot, shoving my torso seaward to avoid the greater depth behind the bar. There was no time to cinch up the lacing at the top of my parka; no time to put more than a piece of seaworm on a hook; no time to smoke; no time to spike the baited rod. Walking was becoming more difficult, the sea was pulling for the back, the chill was getting to me, and I could no longer understand Muff's voice above the roar of the water. *Jesus,* I thought, *when the hell are we getting out of here?*

I could feel the mush of what remained of my seaworms against my chest and the stringer felt like an anchor that I was sure was about to drown me. Each time a wave broke, its force pulled violently on the stringer toward the deeper water behind. I didn't want to catch another bass. All the while that bastard was adding more. The rod in my hand was dead, no doubt the bait gone, and I was too scared to bait it because it was all I could do to hold position in a surf that was now breaking behind us.

"Let's go kid, this way."

Muff took long steps down the beach, studying the alignment of the rigs on the shore. Once we had gone a couple of hundred feet, we edged toward the beach and I could feel the water shallowing as another wave broke against my back, the pressure on my bladder relieving itself involuntarily, mixing with the surf that found itself in my waders. I wanted to kiss the dry beach as I hauled on the heavy rope with one arm, the two tangled surfrods in the other.

Muffy gave me half the load, probably 100 pounds, and let me keep the rope. Then he told me how to get to the dock where I could sell them. At 20 cents a pound, the money would cover the cost of worms and gas for the rest of the week. Had I still been a weekender, it would have covered two trips. We couldn't eat all that fish!

CHAPTER 2

Plugging the Beach

All fishing undergoes change from time to time. Any given year it might be *the* thing to troll, then all of a sudden it is silly to drag a lure behind a boat when everybody knows that live bait is best. How such change comes about is beyond me. When we first arrived at Nauset Beach, the regulars all spoke longingly about the good old days of when everybody plugged the beach. Then, they said, buggies plied the track point to point to lay Atoms into the surf until bass were located. "Point to point," was a term so often used that I think the saying was the very first thing I ever heard about striper fishing that bored me. My feelings were that if plug fishing was so exciting, so compelling, what the hell are you doing getting fat beside baited rods? Full length of the beach you would see campers, with up to eight rods spiked beside them, and nobody around, the old man inside eating or even sound asleep with his wife trained to look out the window occasionally to make sure one of them wasn't down hard with the take of a bass.

But bait fishing is too slow for somebody who bursts with energy and is also out for the buck. After sliding 40 cents worth of worms on the hook, you walk 200 feet in a shallow surf, lay into it and half the meat splats in the suds behind you. Then you wait a half-hour, without realizing that a million little critter things that live in the ocean have polished the hook and that you weren't fishing at all. When plug fishing, the strike comes to the hand and you always know that you are fishing. After all, not all nights are like that on which Muff educated me. But there was so much bottom fishing being done on Nauset that the gorgeous tide rip of Chatham Inlet was a no man's land. Unsuitable for worming because the fast water there pushed even an eight ounce sinker against the beach within minutes, only a handful of regulars ever showed there. These were mostly loners who plugged and who didn't fish with families, passing the campers with headlights out late in the tide. Mostly the names I mentioned earlier, real surfcasters, who didn't knuckle under to fishing styles, who already knew how they wanted to fish. Moreover, for them it was not "point to point," it was surfcasting as they knew it. Men like Charley Murat.

He ran a custom tackle shop in Rhode Island where he wound the finest surf rods of the time. He was an old-timer, in his sixties, no money problems, happy about life, kids grown, short, overweight, had a round face and smiled more than most. Charley was good to our oldest, talking more to the kid than he would anybody else. He would put his arm around our son, giggle in a way that for him was a personal calling card, and ask Dickie when he was going to get a 40 pounder. By the time Dickie was 10 he had a Murat schoolie rod, a little eight foot thing, one piece, that had a 710 reel taped to the butt with 10 pound mono. Theirs was that old man/little boy relationship that we've all seen so much of, one that a father so enjoys which raises no threat. Maybe, that is what I want to think because Charley and I were never very thick. Maybe he didn't want to appear too friendly for fear that the greater number of his customers might be watching. Still, I was a customer too so he stayed on the line, his distance.

While at the barber shop, I had read about an angler in Finland who carved some plugs out of balsa wood. When I asked Charley if he had any Rapalas in the shop, he scolded me as to why I wanted to fish that crap when the darter and dropper would catch all the bass you could ever want. That was

Moving on to Chatham Inlet, a mile South of Long Bar, we found obliging stripers that hung in the rips taking plugs and eels.

one thing about old Charley, he wasn't going to change, not the old master. I had to throw big money elsewhere for a couple of them. The Rapalas were weak, cast lousy, and made you think too often about their cost, but did they ever look like a baitfish and did they ever catch schoolies.

The low tide fishing that Muff had taught me had gotten me to thinking about where the bass went when the water was deep enough to drive us off the bar. One night, after everybody had finished, the water only a couple of hours short of flood, I slipped out of the buggy to cast the hole behind Long Bar. I hadn't been there but a few minutes when I heard a few slurps of feeding fish along with regular takers that would engulf the plug like it was candy. I know that I could have taken some with any of the traditional plugs, but never in the number as with these little cigars, which looked so much like sand eels. It was so easy that you could take as many schoolies plugging as might be caught the earlier four hours of the rise on worms. I already knew that from high tide to when the inlet slacked, a period of 2½ hours, the plugging there was best. Moreover, with the plugs you could fish the beach in hippers without worrying about drowning. The flaw in worming so late into the tide was that there had to be a slot in time where fish would be packed away before anybody saw them, tackle conversions from bait fishing to plugging, and maybe a few minutes to eat. There was so much more fishing to be had and all these people were taking in a mere fraction of it. It seemed that there were two cults in evidence who each practiced their own craft, oblivious to the other. Why not be a part of both?

When you are on the beach for the summer you tend to forget what day it is, only knowing it is a weekend by the number of surfcasters on the beach. I was really putting fish in the box with the double plan. One night I had so much action that I roused Dickie out of bed—he was about 10 at the time but a worthy caster with the little stick Charley had given him—and we topped off every cooler in the buggy. I found it so enjoyable and productive that I didn't want to quit just because the tide was slacking. Joyce and the girls were asleep but all I had to do in preparation to moving the truck was stand the coffee pot in the sink. When we got to the inlet, a drive of about a mile, I couldn't believe that the place was devoid of all fishermen.

Because of the constriction to the opening in Chatham Inlet, the tide still roars toward the inside well past when it has stopped behind Long Bar. Thus, at high tide on the chart our plugs were drumming in the current and they didn't do that very long before a bass would come behind it to pull it down. I was fighting one when I saw Dickie backing with one of his own. After clubbing mine, I handed him my rod and finished bringing his in. While bending over his to remove the plug, I heard the drag on the reel he was fishing. At that rate there were always two fish being handled and because there was nobody around we let the fish lay all over the beach. By dawn we had as many bass to pick up and pack as we had in the coolers that we had filled bait fishing on Long Bar and plugging behind it! Take a look at the arithmetic: The night's take was between 500 and 600 pounds, a little over half of which was in coolers that didn't have any more ice. The last price we had been paid was 20 cents per pound which meant that we had well over $100 worth, which was about what I cleared in a week teaching machine shop. Think of it, a week's pay in one night for playing. Then there were the logistics: Over 200 pounds were in plastic bags in the aisle of the buggy, it would be 90 degrees today, the fish would start stinking by noon, Joyce and the girls were tripping on them, and the round trip to the fish pier would take four hours. We left the inlet just after sunrise because I don't sleep well with things hanging over me.

When we got to the dock there was only one tub trawler unloading cod, red eyed lumpers hanging around. One of them helped us offload the fish from the buggy and Dickie shoveled crushed ice into the coolers after rinsing them. I folded the the receipt for 540 pounds into my wallet and left. Going through Orleans I kept trying to think of what had been wrong with how Dickie and I had handled the blitz. For one thing he handled my larger surf-rod as well as he did his own smaller one. This meant that he could cast any of them if he had to. Our total supply of Rapalas was down to four, because I had lost one setting on a fish behind the bar. It seemed to me that with the kind of money we had just dropped at the dock that it was poor business to go back there short of anything. And, with all our coolers topped off with ice, where would we put tonight's take without throwing ice away? Painfully, I put part of the nights profits into three more plugs that had been carved by that genius from Finland and a cooler that might stretch our stay on the beach an extra day. Dickie checked the trash dumpster for discarded seaworms while I aired out the buggy, coming back with enough to keep us in bait the rest of the week.

About half way down the beach, the radiator ready to boil over, we shut down into the wind and all slept. By sunset we were awake enough to finish the run down to Long Bar. Joyce cooked a big meal and the boy and I readied tackle by tying Rapalas to all the spinning rods before standing a pair of 9 foot conventionals in their sand spikes. It was full dark by the time we were finished eating causing us to be a little late getting on the bar.

The water hadn't risen yet when we put out bait and things were a little slow. Moreover, the rods jiggled occasionally from small stuff, probably pollock. By 10:00 P.M. Dickie was sagging both from the monotony and the wearing of the night before so I sent him off to bed. An hour later, just as I was about to reel in the gear myself, a schoolie took the most distant line causing me to hang in a little longer but there was no further action. With Long Bar slow there seemed little point in casting plugs behind it so I drove on down to the inlet where a small rip had begun to form. Once I was certain where the truck was I killed the headlights, swung the buggy door out of the wind, shut down, and removed a few shovels of sand from the left front wheel to level our quarters.

Against the dim and distant lights of Chatham I could see the dark stain of the rip, making an occasional change in its shades of gray here and there as though some form of life were disturbing it. Stripers. The sliver of balsa drifted briefly until the mono tightened. Then it moved across current, digging slightly, until I dropped the tip to ease its frantic motion and then a stain upset it, missed, and settled out of sight. Casting again to the same spot, I sought to repeat the enticing path and motion, but before I could execute my plan a bass engulfed it pulling the tip of the rod down as line slid from the drag. Unlike the schoolies we had taken most of the summer, this fish made runs that stripped 100 feet off the reel at a time causing me to follow into Pleasant Bay a good 200 yards downtide of the rip. Then I beached the lineside that was in the mid-twenties dragging it back. There were a few pops in the rip after that but as the tempo of the rising water increased the tip seemed to become more devoid of fish.

For most of the night I sipped coffee listening for signs that some might be coming through as I walked the beach with a rod, but the store was closed. Rinsing the pair of fish of all sand, I packed them away in the ice, lay beside Joyce in my jeans, and slept until noon.

At the time there was so much bottom fishing done at Nauset that the rip at Chatham Inlet was a no man's land.

Our first four wheel drive, a FC-170 Jeep with heretofore unknown mobility. No more pushing!

CHAPTER 3

Turning Commercial

The afternoon sou'west came up stronger than usual, blowing so hard as to cover the track. I had to move the truck around to get the door into the lee and the girls came in complaining that the sand was stinging their feet and legs. Gusts were well over 50 but the sustained wind layed a fog-like pall of airborne sand over the beach making it difficult to see even with clear skies. In spite of this I could make out a number of birds working at the inlet at about the time when the tide would be just beginning to make up for the bay. These I watched for some time with binoculars until Dick came in out of breath saying that he had seen them as well. You had only to turn your head from it for a few minutes then look back to discern an increase in their number. Now the terns and herring gulls numbered in the thousands, wheeling and diving frantically. We started the truck.

To me it felt as though there were something wrong with the vehicle because it failed to respond to acceleration. Unlike our usual movements, we lacked the benefit of a track; moreover, the blunt nose of the van was being held back by the wind and our progress was about equal to walking speed. Dickie was looking through the glasses yelling, "Faster, Dad, faster," the truck, losing power until I dropped it into the lowest gear, one which is never used. Mom and the girls glared at the sight as we approached painfully slowly, the birds pounding the water without regard for our presence. Dick was out the door before the wheels stopped turning and I was pulling rods off the side of the truck when I heard him call.

The water was white, so churned up from the wind that you couldn't make out the current. Large sheets of baitfish, appearing brown, pock-marked the short areas of green between the foamers, and you could make out the dusky shaded bodies of stripers lashing through them. Carol, who knew nothing of how to handle a surfrod, was backing away from the water with Dickie's rod while he ran back for another. The Rapalas normally would have been worthless to this gale because even a casting champion couldn't have thrown one more than 20 feet. But distance had no meaning as the bass were everywhere. The twins, who were three at the time, cheered when Mom walked hers away from the surf in the same way Carol had, and Dickie was hauling his on the last wave. We had 20 pounds of stripers flopping on the sand and I hadn't made a cast yet! Lashing the baitfishing rig from the big stick, I rolled the mono through the eye of an Atom plug and delivered our last available line. It drifted in the current while I reeled up the wind-slack and I set on number four.

All the expensive, little Finland plugs stayed in the first fish as I cut lines and tied snap-swivels to them; then I clipped on Darters, Atoms, Kastmasters—anything laying around the buggy. But our soon to be professional team was lacking in casters and the retrievers had a long way to go. Nonetheless, in spite of their inexperience, dozens of school bass were strewn about the shore by sunset. All the boxes of ice had nearly melted away, the wind responsible for much of it, and the boy and I were able to pack everything safely away for tomorrow's trip to town.

Coming back to the inlet from town under a high, late July sun had been a grueling and sweaty trip, the temperature close to 100. I had warned the kids about opening the back window of the buggy. At the low speeds of the beach the CO from the truck exhaust can invade the living quarters. But to

Sandra, one of our babies and a real fisherwoman at age seven.

Many years later, Sandra at age 16. We had one close call with her I will never forget.

kids it is difficult to envision a danger that remains so invisible as the exhaust of the vehicle. The heat of the day was so oppressive that they cranked the window open to relieve part of the misery of so many hours on the trail. When we arrived at Long Bar all of them bounded out in their bathing suits as they always do for a swim—all but one. Joyce didn't want her to sleep in this heat and went aft to rouse her but she was unconscious. Overcome by truck exhaust, our Sandra, our baby, last by three minutes, her breathing shallow, her skin clammy to the touch, eyes rolled back, was on the edge of death. I carried her limp, little 35 pound frame out into the open for air as her brother and sisters stared in astonishment.

Joyce began to pray:

"Hail Mary, full of grace, the Lord is with thee ..."

Dickie began to whimper out of fear, out of a sense of urgency that he could read in his mother and father. Susan and Carol then felt it when they saw him. Laying her on a beach towel, I watched strands of her blond hair lift in the barely perceptable flow of air that brushed past her. She was dying.

I can't recall how much time passed because it has always been a thing that I seek to put out of my mind. I remember that we wrapped some ice in a towel and placed it upon her forehead, that we tried to let as much of the sou'west as we could get to her face, that we prayed, that we cried. I remember that it crossed my mind that my greed was at fault. Maybe that is where I was when her eyes opened and she began to cry. As long as I live I will never forget the fear that we all felt, nor the relief when our baby began to cry as she sipped Kool-Aid.

Within minutes she was flopping around in a foot of water behind Long Bar with the others who watched her closely.

The first fish-check we ever got was the relatively small kill with Muffy: a little over 100 pounds, one box, as they say, that paid 25 cents per pound, up a nickel from the price we expected. But that was only a taste. The drop for the previous week, the one where we nearly lost Sandra, had nearly 700 pounds because we had topped off the boxes twice and the price had risen again to 28. I'll never forget the pay-off—$193! That week we more than doubled my teaching take home pay. But it was not all blitz for the entire summer. On alternate weeks, when the tides were wrong, 200 pounds was about all we could do; then we would make it up on the good tides so that the average that first summer came out to around $1000 for the summer. Still, I hadn't started the season expecting to bring in money and the $500 I had hidden in the buggy to get us through was still there along with all the checks for August when we went home Labor Day.

The following winter we chassis mounted a camping trailer to a four wheel drive Jeep, FC-170 pickup and we never pushed again.

With the improved mobility of 4WD, Joyce and I had a more aggressive attitude toward locating stripers. There was a more favorable bunk arrangement for the growing children. We had doubled the number of surfrods to eight, one of which was a custom wrapped "kid's conventional" that Charley had put together for Dickie based upon his size. Murat had measured the boy's height and arm length and determined, to everyone's surprise, that he was 9/10 of a man and that an eight foot rod, with all specifications reduced by 10 percent would fit him perfectly. It was a darling little stick with diamond wraps and carboloy guides and Dickie cast it like a pro. Meanwhile, Joyce had gotten proficient with the spinning gear so that when the fishing was good enough during the day or evening, or especially blitzy in the deep night, she would join us. Carol, who was seven, cost us more in lost lures than she could ever hope to regain by backing from the water with a schoolie; and the twins were so small, that if they forgot to open a bail would end up casting themselves. Still, we had the makings of a small army of surfcasters that could go nowhere but up. One afternoon, when I lay in my bunk stowing sleep for the coming night tide, I could hear Dickie giving casting lessons to his three sisters on the beach. This was a contravention of my orders because I feared damage to the monofilament which I guarded as though it were gold. But I let it go because I had the back-of-the-mind feeling that some good might come from it all. This was, after all, Cape Cod.

In those days commercial fishing was viewed as an honorable vocation that had with it the same aggrarian pride that farmers enjoy—being a food gatherer, a protein provider, a trait or urge natural to man. Don't get me wrong, I was still looking out for number one. However, in this new found life I could play my brains out while bringing fish that were begging to be brought to market. There were uncountable tons of available bass for anyone who could efficiently harvest them. And, it was a case of knowing when to kill yourself and when to ride easy upon your store of energy. All sorts of obstacles lie in wait for anyone who dared believe it would be easy. Bad winds, gunk, neap tides, dogfish, crowds or good old-fashioned simple mindedness could all make the filling of one's fish boxes impossible. You had to be willing to sweat in a gale, pee in your waders, and drive to the dock without sleep to keep a catch table fit. We were!

Painfully, I found out that it was best to be a loner.

CHAPTER 4

The Grapevine

One of the inevitable outcomes of living on the beach for three seasons is that you really learn what is likely to happen and where. Moreover, being there, you become attuned to every run of fish as it relates to tide, wind, light, and weather. The result is an edge over anybody who fishes the beach casually or even rabidly on weekends. Others learn that you know more than they partly because you are rumored to be getting better results and partly—if you are as foolish as I—because you make too many public predictions which hold up. Then, as a young man, I wanted recognition, wanted to be the big torpedo, the expert that everybody relied upon. I never dreamed that I would someday loathe the day that I had been such a responsive, cooperative guide for so many on Nauset Beach.

That July, 1967, I'll guess, I met a guy very much like ourselves who fished with a wife and small kids during his vacation. We got friendly because I had stopped my truck coming back from town and gaffed a 35 pounder for him. We had a couple of beers in his buggy and I urged him to come up to the inlet that night. But he, feeling that bait fishing had more promise, wanted us to stay and fish behind Long Bar with him. The result of our friendly disagreement was that we would report the previous night's fishing to each other the next day, that we could mutually benefit from a knowledge of where the stripers had shown.

I can attest that the fish didn't show at the inlet and I did so when I saw him. And he, lamenting that they just didn't come in anywhere, said that they hadn't had a hit.

That evening an acquaintance came down to the inlet, asked about the fishing, then expressed surprise at how poor I said it was. Pointing to the buggy where he had just stopped, he told me he saw the catch of my new found friend that had taken 50 schoolies the night before behind Long Bar—all on Rapalas, the very plug that I had so promoted. The guy had a pretty good thing going for himself: He would have the benefit of my fishing without upholding his end of the agreement. I've never forgiven him.

Weekends was when the pressure was on me to lend a hand. There was one guy who ran an inland tackle shop who always came on Saturday afternoon for one night. Business constraints kept him from fishing anymore than that. One week he would start fishing at sunset and Joyce and I kept him in coffee and hot food all the night. On the alternate week, when the tide was late, I would rouse him early enough to suit up and drink the coffee that I always handed him. I treated him like a brother, lining him up for the right time, urging him to remove hardware on nights when the fire was too bright, coaching him through schools of bass the whole season. He had it knocked because to him manhood was a buggy full of fish and being in the tackle business it was important that he brag of his successes.

I should have seen it earlier, should have smelled that something was wrong. The inlet had its regular visitors whom I knew. Why, I began to wonder, did total strangers always show up on Sunday night but rarely any other night? Worse, the Sunday night people were always on vacation and if they hit fish I had them under my arm for the better part of two weeks. It had never occurred to me that roughly one of five of all the buggies on the beach were staying. And the fellow who I had been helping would stop at every rig on the way off the beach to show off his catch. Worse, most of the time what he was showing were not even his because he would take in fish for me, which was often a reflection of the whole family. The guy not only bragged, hurting me in the process, but he was showing the take of four people and representing it as his own. Most often the fishing wasn't any way near what he led people to believe. I don't care who he says caught them, but did he have to tell the truth about where?

That's how we ended up with the Jersey bunch every year, though I can't say that it turned out that bad. These guys come in, six buggies all together, like the friggin' Third Armored. Nice four-wheelers, all new stuff. These guys had so much dough that they were spending interest. Shut the trucks off, pop open the beer cans and yell, "Who's Frank Daignault?" they did. It made me feel that I was going to be used with class. No beating around the bush, one guy shoves a beer at me, holds out his hand and shakes it like we were old buddies. They were all around me talking like they came from another world that had no "R"s (the boids is woikin') excited about the fishing, asking questions: What time? Can we hold bottom here? Any bluefish? These guys either truly believed that I was going to be glad to see them or they anticipated my resistance and had decided to bury it with good, old-fashioned blarney. They were tired from a day and half on the road, deprived because they came from "Joisey," and depraved because they suffered from the inscrutable love of striper fishing.

"Rapalas at sunset," I told them, "no wire leaders."

That night, in spite of prayers that not a striper would come within miles of the inlet, the linesides roared in like it was the end of the world and them Jersey bastards murdered them. My fish!

To these guys life is a party, especially when the beaches you are in the habit of fishing have either all been closed or so regulated against sleeping that they run everybody off at sunset. During the first lull someone whistled and everybody came out of the water yelling, "Ginger brandy." A Coleman lantern came out glaring all over the inlet, bottles and shot glasses tinkling and them all yelling, "Fraaaank."

"To Frank," one of them hoists, "best goddamned surfcaster ..."

"Hear, hear."

And we all knock down the brandy so the bottle can go around again.

I'll admit that I was naive in those days but I can sniff out a con job, sometimes ... if the wind is right.

"What's next, Frank babe?"

"That's it men," I said, in my most authoritative voice, "they've come through for the night. After a swuaray through the bay they'll cut out around Monomoy and we won't see them again 'til tomorrow, if we're lucky."

I saw the eyes lift, the distrust, how they all seemed to reach for the jug at the same time. It was as though it had come to all of them at once that if they could get enough of the stuff into me I would break loose with where and when they would have the real striper fishing. You don't think I was going to tell them that what came in was going to be going out during the dropping tide, do you?

Excusing myself, I gestured with disdain at the brandy and went to bed. After an hour, the water pulling for the outside, I slipped out of the buggy, noticed their shadows behind one of the larger trucks, and headed on foot for this end of Long Bar. Once there, I recognized the tips of at least six surf-rods following over the brow of the beach, their bodies out of sight. Confident that they were watching, I started casting with a will ... in six inches of water.

"Caught ya, ya somnabitch!" as they all ran down to the water like they had discovered gold, casting like the Boston girls had the tow-rope.

I laughed so out of breath that I felt the brandy come up on me and they, still retrieving hungrily, expecting a hit any minute, were setting as their plugs dug in to the little waves of sand on the bottom.

One by one they left the water as they realized what I had done to them, laughing as much as I and we all went back to the buggies in the lightness of school boys to finish up the brandy.

The experience with the Jersey bunch was something that I was never to reconcile; you know that you end up being used by every budding surfcaster who has ever heard your name. It becomes necessary to guard your flanks, to keep a low profile, minimize your successes, say as little as possible, shun even the friendliest smile. But there is a side of you that knows that some among them are so worthwhile, so beautiful, that there is so much that they can give. Sometimes you think you can tell who is worth trusting, like the Jersey gang. Still, your sense of betrayal is heightened by the memory of those you've mistakenly trusted. Thus, just as I had mistakenly established a reputation for helping many people out, I learned—from the earlier examples above—that it was time to become known for being a silent, uncooperative loner. Years later, in a letter that Frank Woolner wrote to me about Cape Cod surfcasting, he said that he had heard that I was the bastard of the beach. He could have paid me no greater compliment.

My dear friend, the late Charley Murat in his shop where he made fishing rods from unlimited tuna to little one handers. We loved him and somehow envied the way he died. Photo courtesy of Dave Hammock.

CHAPTER 5

Requiem for a Surfman

Marked by year class after year class of successful Chesapeake reproduction, the sixties were burgeoning years for striped bass. The fish were virtually everywhere and word spread rapidly throughout the Striper Coast of both good fishing and the fantasia of beach life on Cape Cod. Hundreds of homemade buggies sprang out of backyard workshops along with new pickups with campers on them. Meanwhile pressure was mounting on surfcasting beaches in New York, New Jersey, and Rhode Island to kick the "squatters" off the beaches for environmental reasons. Opponents of the buggies argued that the vehicles were destroying the beach grass which hastened erosion. Of course the true reason for wanting to get the fishermen out was as ignoble for the opponents as it was self-indulgent for the surfmen: each simply wanted the resource for themselves. One by one beaches to the south fell. East Beach, Charlestown, R.I. was parceled off for cottage lots, largely bought up by surfcasters. Places we had never seen like Breezy Point, Fire Island and all the Jersey shore became memories, forcing surfcasters there to Cape Cod. The National Park Service had taken over all the Outer Cape from Eastham north even hoping to wrest control of Nauset Beach from Orleans and Chatham, though this met with no success. In the mind's eye of most surfmen, whatever happened elsewhere, there would always be the Seashore Park because that was the Federal government, which, unlike the towns, could not pass regulations that discriminated against outsiders.

The good fishing tripled the number of buggies causing the town fathers of Orleans and Chatham to introduce controls. First, a permit system associated with a limit upon the number of vehicles on the beach was instituted. But this had no effect upon the allure of the shore and use continued to grow. In Chatham expensive shore front homes had their seascape view of Nauset Beach marred by the sight of 200 trucks lined up on Long Bar and sprinkled about Chatham Inlet. Controls were not working and apparently officials sought to make the beach less attractive by limiting campers to 24 hours. It was an aggravation game that most of us prayed would not work. Thus, each morning we drove the full length of the beach, renewed our permits, and drove it again.

It was during one of these trips that we learned how much the beach fisherman was despised in Chatham. Early afternoon, while passing the Old Harbor Coast Guard Station, I waved at the bathers there the way it had always been the custom. Only this time they were not responding. They were spread for several hundred feet, some in the water, others on blankets, watching. But today all were without the customary smiles. Icy. I had heard that the buggies had become unpopular, but this was the first time that I could feel it. Pressing it, I tooted the horn and waved excitedly. More ice. Still, most were looking at us in spite of their reluctance to respond to my artificial friendliness.

The Track!

Under power the truck lurches if the clutch is depressed. Thus, there is never need to use the brakes on the sand. When I threw the clutch we stopped quickly, Susan sliding forward into the window screen from the top bunk, the others pitching harmlessly upon the abundant bedding inside. I know that Joyce was looking for a board with nails on it when the decaying snow

One of the joys of those days on the beach was having a friend like
Charley who was a surfcaster. Photo courtesy of Dave Hammock.

fence and pages of the *New York Times* gave way under her weight. Falling forward in the tank-trap, perhaps two feet deep, she looked at me in astonishment as I went to her. When I looked at the beach people all were facing the sea.

That was the first time that I felt the pressure of local resistance to the buggies. Of course, everybody on the beach was talking about the towns getting ready to run the fishermen off. Charley Murat had bought a home in Orleans because he had seen it coming. I had told him about the incident with the hole in the track. "Bad," he said. Charley and his one word sentences. One time, when I couldn't start my truck, he looked at the wires and proclaimed like a man of science, "Wet." If you brought in a striper that was a little bigger than what was being taken, "Good." Sure, if he was excited about something, you might get a short sentence, but he wasn't one for stringing a whole bunch of words together. Yet, there was an inscrutable charm to the old guy. I know that he helped me a lot, made me feel good around the shop when some old guard of the time got to talking down to me back when I was new to the beach. It was Charley that brought me the plugs I needed. Charley always pleaded for moderation whenever anybody got a little out of line. And Charley was the surfcaster's surfcaster not because of the night he took four cows all over 49 at Monomoy and five others over 40 in a day when a 50 pounder made you famous. His charm was his simplicity. When the fish were in the surf he would walk an eel down the beach allowing it to move with the tide freely instead of retrieving it like the others. When jointed eels were hot he made them for us. When our fishing reels broke, he repaired them. When we needed another surfrod, how long? And when our spirits waned, he revitalized us.

The year he turned 70 we had talked about the towns, watching the sunset together. The old boy knew that he was not well and that surfcasting is a game of endurance. Moreover, he had been warned when a mild seizure had overtaken him a couple of years before. Seeming defiant about his health, he had even said to me that night:

"If I can't fish, I might just as well die."

So he fished and worked at the same headlong pace and I think he knew what it could do to him, but he was caught up in a lifetime of what he loved and the Nauset Beach that was as dear. That's where he was the last night of his life.

Everybody was into fish when he came down the beach. Mostly Woonsocket Striper Club boys, they called to him as they ran to rods that bowed east under the strain. The old man tried to seem casual as he hurried down to the surfline. Five of his disciples were close by—fishing furiously— when Charley caught his first.

"Aha!" he chided, "the old man's gonna show ya again!"

One of the gang hooked up.

"But mine's bigger!"

To the left another angler leaned into a bull striper.

The pace was feverish; almost everyone had fish on. By now, Charley was landing his second—a 20 pounder and he called: "Beat that fellas!" He made another cast and hung another right off. The Cape sun had lowered enough to lengthen shadows, and suddenly it was evening.

It was the third fish.

One of the men turned in time to see Charley tumble face down on the beach, the rod made by the master's own hands sliding under his shoulder on the wet sand—alive with the thrashing weight of a big striped bass. A wave rose, stretched toward the shore, broke into foam and annointed our

Charley.

Word traveled on Long Bar and the burly characters there could only sob; another tucked his long billed swordfisherman's cap under his arm and prayed. His friends stood in a tight circle around the body; for them time had stopped.

Then, an orphaned rod standing in its spike groaned under the strain of a bass surging away with the bait. A caster turned instinctively heading for the pounding stick.

"Cut that goddamned line," someone shouted. But before anyone could move all the rods were leaning to the east, each tied into a hooked striper.

"Cut them all," the voice commanded. One of the boys that Charley had tutored walked through the stand of surfrods lancing the taut line on every one. Five sticks snapped straight in the last fire of sunset.

Word spread like fire all along the Cape. We'll never know if it was he or the way he went that caused anglers to whisper of his passing over the gunwales of their surfboats or at every hotspot where surfmen gather. He died with two fish on the beach and another cartwheeling wildly out there on a darkening sea. Having had a warm sun over his shoulder, his last impressions must have been the softness of clean sand and the sweet song of the high surf.

There are some of us who envy him.

CHAPTER 6

Off to P-Town

1970. I was 34, Joyce was a college student, Dickie was 13, Carol was 10 and the twins were nine—everybody a competent caster. The situation at Nauset had so deteriorated that the nearest thing to total banishment had come: a regulation that required buggy users there to absent themselves for 72 hours upon completion of a maximum of 72 hours on the beach. The three days on, three days off business killed vacationers and regulars like us. There had been some more tank trappings, one putting a surfcaster's wife into the windshield busting her nose. Townies were hostile toward outsiders like us and it seemed stupid to risk encounters or knock yourself out on the fish, get their number, then have to leave for three days and lose touch with the school. Even if we continued at Nauset we still needed an alternate beach on which to kill three days. Having heard so much of the striper fishery there, P-Town was the obvious place to fill our needs, where mobile sport fishermen were considered part of local culture. There the Park Service had guaranteed that they had no intention of altering the charm of entrenched customs. Their mission, they said, was to preserve Cape Cod and enhance multiple use of the Seashore Park.

The contrast of Provincetown with the conservative, quaint, communities of Orleans and Chatham, with which we had become accustomed, astonished us. Narrow crowded streets hosted the shaven heads of Krishna types, people shouted social messages to men holding hands or beaded ladies without underwear wearing gossamer thin dresses of another era. It was both a place of rogues and of those who wanted to see them. The Calcutta like streets were jammed with traffic and humanity bordered by little shops that sold penny candy and strange wares difficult to find anywhere else. In numbers the year round residents were overwhelmed by tourists of summer. Still, you could identify a commercial fisherman by a strapping body, a beard, and a knife on his hip. If you looked closely you almost always could see a fisherman from the beach heading for the dock in a small four-wheeler. Days in town, when bringing in fish or when winds were bad, I liked walking the streets greeting people that I didn't know: "Hey, howya doin'" Afternoons we would drink a few drafts at the Foc'sle and ogle the braless waitresses while watching the commercial fishermen get very drunk. But for all the can-of-worms feel that town had, the air was that of the sea, blowing fresh from the sou'west out of Cape Cod Bay. And while there was a charm, P-Town was the most whacked out place we had ever seen.

There is no true surf on the beach in P-Town. Water is flat from Race Point east to well past High Head. There, once the curve of the Cape comes around to facing east the combers begin to build so that it is water like that of Nauset. Back at the Race, the prevailing sou'west will often kick up a good surf but this is wind blown water. Because of the flat water in the lee of dunes from Race Point to High Head, it is possible to launch a boat from shore on all but foul weather days. There are few places in the world where such launching takes place without the help of an estuary. Typically, the beach fisherman will have a buggy to service the needs of the family; a small trailered boat—anywhere from a 14 foot aluminum to a 20 foot fiberglass hull, many with two motors; and, a chase vehicle which is a small

Carol at age 10 with a fine mackerel. The kids would gather every evening to catch them in 1970, our first year at P-Town

4wd that is used to trailer and push off the boat and make grocery and fish runs to town.

The majority of beach fishermen here are boatmen who fish by day. However, there is a small, by comparison, number of surfcasters who cling tenaciously to surfcasting tradition. This is a proud group of night fishermen, who wander the beach with a small four-by and who—to use their words—would rather have a sister in a whorehouse than a friend in a boat.

The surfcaster's routine, as we found it, was to fish the "Back Beach," three or four miles east, on the incoming then scoot to the "Second Rip" at the top of the tide. This was about the best fishing for two hours down. Curiously, Race Point, with all the fine moving water there, was not part of the surfcaster's itinerary. It didn't make any sense to me that the men of the beach were passing it up, but when I asked the formula answers were that the water was too shallow and that the prevailing sou'west made casting difficult. Yet, the boats jigged their wire with jigged eels within shouting distance and brought boxes of cows daily to the dock. For all the fish that were killed in the boats, the surfcasting in P-Town was no where near what it had been at Nauset. Yet, I found myself being taken in by the charm of the place, particularly the surfcasters there.

All of my brief surfcasting life I had never known more than a handful of truly dedicated casters—Charley, the Jersey bunch and maybe a few others. The others were slackers who fed off information from the guys who plugged their brains out. But here the mere ownership of waders was *prima facie* evidence of dedication and the best of them were the "New Yorkers." Typically, the Massachusetts fishermen viewed the New Yorkers with a kind of desperate resentment; the big city boys made we locals insecure whenever they were around, which was almost all the time. New Yorkers are sharp—streetwise as they say. They were viewed as aggressive, overly pushy, who took anything that they wanted for a piece of the beach to fish from. We country bumpkins failed to understand that a New Yorker, from the time that he can walk away from his mother for more than two minutes, is competing for space, for air, for transportation. True, because of who I am, and where I come from, there is more Massachusetts in me than New York. And at first I did not trust them, nor understand their aggressive behavior anymore than others of the world who have known them. But they had a thing going for them that endeared me right from the beginning: the same inscrutable love for surfcasting, at the same intensity, as I.

Among the roughly 50 New Yorkers, some had been fishing the beach there since the 40's. We younger men—and there were some from N.Y.— emulated and admired the old guard who employed a system of hunt and cast with squidding reels. These they attached to an eleven foot stick with which they cast 45-pound micron braid. The big Atom swimmer was *the* plug, particularly if you had some of the old, pre-51 models manufactured when the tools were new. Bob Pond had shifted his production efforts then to spinning size plugs to the dismay and chagrin of these staunch traditionalists. Stan Gibbs Lures still made big plugs along with Creek Chub with their marvelous Giant Pikie Minnow, which was fondly known as the "jointed eel." In spite of the disdain that spinning tackle drew, just about all the younger guys used it while they worked at the transition to conventional reels. But the one method that truly characterized the New Yorker was use of the rigged eel. These were selected for size, say 16 inches, killed kosher, then strung with two 9/0 salmon hooks (Siwash) and pumped rhythmically in the rips. No thanks to them, I had to learn to rig myself. There was no bait

Chase vehicle launching a boat in P-Town. To us this was a strange place.

fishing done from the beach. Also, teasers were unheard of.

We marveled at the weird, do-your-own-thing world that we had discovered at the tip of Cape Cod. The sand was more difficult to get around on but that was compensated for by the short beach and easy ride to town for dropping fish and buying groceries. Deep water was near us for the first time. We had never seen whales close in to the beach but here they frolicked in the Race, blowing water high not a tenth of a mile from shore. Great schools of mackerel came down the beach every night at sunset causing all the children to run from the campers with trout tackle to blitz their brains out. Having never seen them under two pounds they were impressive enough to hammer any spoon that was placed before them then run line from a reel. These were not sold, mostly kept cool for striper bait; perhaps a few were eaten.

There had been much talk about bluefish because the regulars there were hoping for them to come as they had the year before. These seemed the only hope for surf action because P-Town was mired in an awful striper drought. Boats came in with a 30 pounder here or there but the surfmen were dying. Nonetheless, we all went through the motions each night, but there was more standing around breezing or nodding in the buggy cabs. We longed for the monster bluefish that we had heard of the year before when they had been taken up to 19 pounds. Something that you have to keep in mind is that there were not the choppers then that we have had since, particularly from shore. If you did catch one anywhere it was five or six pounds. Then the World Record was 24 change, taken in the Azores. Talk of such monsters so close made me suspect.

It was late July, maybe a 1:00 A.M. tide, another boring shape up of regulars, about half of them New York. Some of us hadn't been tight in weeks when the newly arrived bluefish came through. You could mark their progress in the rip, coming down from the Race, as we set, fanned and cursed, about half hooking up. But it didn't matter because if your plug survived the first whack, three cranks later your tip would be hauled into the water. On average they ranged 15 to 18 pounds, with one runt that was 12 that caught a lot of attention because many had never seen one that small. As fresh migrants the fish were all lean and within a few weeks you could add two pounds to everything that we had taken the first night.

These P-Town guys were such torpedoes, swaggering about all their surf-casting accomplishments. You should have seen them backlashing and popping off when those first bluefish came through; they had forgotten how to fish! Imagine fishing a month, waiting for the blitz to come, then blowing it because you forgot how to fish. For my family and me this was high drama because we had been bored with six years of school bass, only an occasional fish big enough to take line off the reel. While we had made money, we were still sport fishermen at heart. Having a new kind of fish, bluefish, brought a real spark to our lives. It was the beginning of what would come to be a season of pull your guts out blitz nightly.

For we commercials the arithmetic was different but there was still a decent bottom line: $15 per box, two boxes a night four nights a week. It was slightly under teacher money but it bought the gas, groceries and gear. The price is still that today because the species is everywhere and the market is flooded. Then, most of the bluefish at Fulton Street came from P-Town. The situation was so reliable that I parked the camper closer to the water so that I could pound on the side of the rig when I hooked up. Having draped 20 plugs on the front of the buggy, the kids would stand on a beached fish and unsnap the lure for another. Close to the water line, we could gut and pack

We were suspicious of New Yorkers at first but our common ground soon made us friends.

with ease. On the right tides, with any kind of wind, it was duck soup.

One night I caught a goosefish, (angler or tails) that ate a loaded Atom 40. Lordy, are those things ever ugly! They are a mouth the size of a patio table with a tail. But I found out later that that tail is a delicacy. Another fellow caught one also and he left his to rot on the beach. Throwing them both into the box, I reasoned that I was taking in blues anyway and marketed them both. Was I ever surprised that my two goosefish brought as much money as a box of blues.

Another night, when the wind quartered out of the nor'west, live squid washed up from the Race clear around to the Traps. After picking a couple for bait, just in case something was chasing, I started kicking them back. But the dumb things would swim right back onto the beach without anything chasing them. Feeling stupid helping them as there were a million, all bent upon the same suicide, I banged on the side of the buggy, my cash register dinging. The girls all came running out, panties and pajamas, grabbing rods and running to the water before I could instruct them on the fine art of the squid picking. Also, the split for this session was no money for the buggy. What the dock paid for the squid was theirs. It was nearly daybreak and when the first light bathed the beach you should have seen those girls, locks of blond hair hell west and crooked, screaming and laughing, squirting squid ink in each other's faces; and did they ever stink! Price turned out to be four cents. Good thing I stopped them at 97 pounds. They split the $3.90 four ways and blew every cent on penny candy and pizza.

Some nights the squid would wash right up on the beach.

At the top of the tide big bluefish would come down from the Race to test our tackle. There were many blitzes with fine surfcasters.

CHAPTER 7

The Race

The error in our first year at the whacked out cloudland to the north was that we had allowed the bluefish to divert our attention from what we should have been learning. As I look back, this was a crucial time in my life because I was coming to the realization that what was learned was far more important than what was caught. You could come upon a hole where the sand eels had dug in, a place where no man has ever caught a striper, and make the killing of your life. You might even laugh all the way to the bank, counting it for the easy money that it was. But the way such a kill can seize a positive hold upon the mind is that you never again pass the spot without checking it out because you remember the night that was so good. Yet, a few minutes here a few minutes there, always to no avail, added up over the years, and time saps your energy to the point where you wish to hell that you had never known the place. The failing of such a situation is that nothing was known to experience it, and nothing was learned as a result of it. Not that I would turn down such one shot deals, but they must be kept in perspective.

But I was going to say more about the growth of the mind. Once, on a small kill of fish back on Nauset's Pleasant Bay I had experienced particular delight, more in fact than with bigger catches. It was as though an inner self was acknowledging the discovery while the conscious me counted everything in pounds. Then, I was too green to understand what my inner mind was already celebrating—that I had learned something. Blindly, I staggered through my youthful formation without recognizing such deposits of fact that would later come to great use. Here we must say the things about learning that many of us know because to fail to acknowledge them would be both a travesty upon order as we examine knowledge, and, deprive the young of the important stepping stones of good reasoning. A load of fish is a fleeting thing that can be stolen while you sleep or by the manipulation of the price. A honey hole for stripers can be changed by one storm; or, it can be ruined by a crowd that has too many friends. But what you know, gentle, patient reader, is yours as long as you still have your mind.

I knew better than to believe the regulars when they said the Race was unsuitable for surfcasting. Not that they were lying, though they were capable of that; but more because they were dull of mind. Certainly, if they were lying they would have been fishing it themselves. Truth is that we were the most recent victims of the traditions that had hog-tied them for 30 years. We didn't find the Race through logic or good sense. I just never trusted it because it was too much like my old Chatham Inlet. Moreover, I misread P-Town surfcasters as too capable to let the Race languor unfished when it was among the finest surfcasting spots on the planet. It is a mistake to believe that others will see what is upon the end of their nose just as surely as it is to believe that you know everything. One of the joys in all fishing is uncovering the truth, whether it is hidden by man or God. Well, He sure was sitting on a pile of striped bass at the Race.

Our first year we used to sleep at the Race because it was a quiet spot to escape the noise of the Second Rip where we all did our casting. The Race crowd was a boat bunch, kind of layed back, that only launched on calm days. No surfcasters. At high tide we would slip down through the Traps,

Race City with its gaggle of buggies, chase vehicles and boats. On a dropping tide with a strong southwest wind there would be fish right there.

making a few casts along the way, then join the bluefish crowd. But every two weeks, when the high tides were at daylight, we didn't bother because even though the water might pull well, the rips were too bright for surf-casting. During such moon phases we stuck out the Race experimenting as to what could be done there. Nothing was happening anywhere else anyway.

The waters of Cape Cod Bay change their direction of sweep four times per day in a mechanical sibilance that cooks miles of exposed salt flats under the summer sun. From Wellfleet to Barnstable the heat brings renewal to microscopic marine life that is gorged upon by blankets of sand eels. These dig in to wet sand, lest they be exposed to predation or the sear-ing heat of the sun. Then, when the flood returns, these thin whisps again gorge upon protein that our eyes cannot see.

At the west edge of the Bay's opening there is no clear, defined geographical prominence to mark where it begins. But to the east the hook of Cape Cod juts into the North Atlantic curving halfway through the com-pass in the effort. Part way through that curve, at its most westerly point, a 200 yard sandbar dips below the high water mark. Another like distance westward, the shallow bottom yields to the incessant tides ending the shoal in a steep submarine banking that does not end until the graph records 90 feet. Mid-tide the surge of water, hurrying to its assigned passage, creates a line of white foam obliquely from the shore where a lighthouse marks its passage. Race Point is the watery home of the ghosts of a thousand fishermen and a hundred once fine vessels.

Days when the prevailing wind blows, the Race lacks the clear definition of a visually defined beginning or end because there is too much sea space for the westerlies to gain momentum. Then, the foamers stack up at Race Bar waiting their turn to pound the shore. Trapped in their grip or perhaps enjoying it, the sand eels scurry from one to another as players in a vicarious game that is for keeps. I know because I have seen a thousand shorebirds wheel and dive over them driving them to the momentary safety of the maelstrom. Then, unaccountably at first, and knowingly later, I learned that something from below was sending them back toward the sky for what might be a more welcome death. I would sit in the shade of my buggy and watch them for hours make their frenzied choice between the avian pluck from above and predatory engulfment from below.

Days when there was a measure of moderation in the wind the boats loafed their engines while the trollers rhythmically swung their bodies from the hip, pulling on the wire that led down. The jigs would surge ahead, then fall to kiss the bottom in a puff of momentarily suspended sand that got no small measure of attention. Bluefish would hip shoot recklessly as the jig passed; and striped bass would stalk for a few yards, timing the movement of the jig, so as to take with precision. Then the boatman would haul back on the short rod and the forces of the sea, the boat, man and fish were con-summated. Some nights, as the flash of Race Light sent its burst westward, you would see a golden sprinkle of sand eels that had moved into the shallows under the cover of darkness. Often you could view a glimpse of what was pushing them. But the best nights were the ones that gave no visual hint of life beyond the littoral boundary, nights when the sou'west piled foam capped seas against the beach, the awesomeness of it all tending to push a caster slightly back, the surf of Race Point became a playground for striped bass and bluefish. Not that it was so simple a situation as waiting for the summer wind to blow. The tide had to be four hours down and your plug had to be swimming in the rips uptide of the bar. And at the slack, a period that can seem desperately short, the bass disperse for 2,000 feet

One of the joys in all fishing is uncovering the truth whether it is hidden by God or man. Well, God was sure sitting on a pile of striped bass at the Race.

clear around to the Traps. Here it is necessary to farm them out yard by yard as they lay in wait of something to kill for dinner. Then, a wrinkle of a rip forms at the Traps building a line from the shore to the north sliding slowly toward the Race. Once it arrives at the bar it stops, then intensifies and the rising water forces the caster back from it so that each fish is perceived to be farther from shore. Truth is that the shore is what is moving.

But they told us that Race Point was a boat fishing place; that it did not yield linesides from the beach; that the wind blew too hard for a caster to lay a plug into favorable water. Pig's ass.

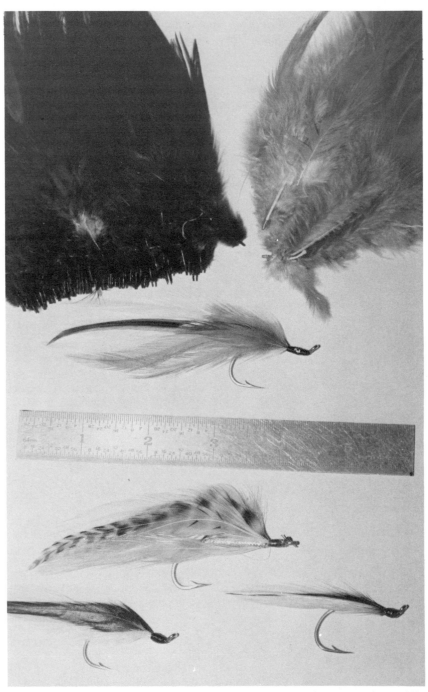

We tied eel flies for use as teasers by lashing down four to seven saddle
hackles on a 2/0 hook. If the wind blew real hard we cast them with sinkers
and cleaned up.

CHAPTER 8

The Weaponry

Anyone who relied upon either wind or the sound of their feeding would never have known of the stripers that slid under Race Light. Appearing like ghosts, their dark green forms were barely visible in the brightness of each revolution. So much so that I wasn't sure the first time, and I impatiently awaited another pass to look again.

By the time I had finished trying all the plugs that usually worked, my attitude was that there was nothing to lose by trying the eel-fly. The weight forward fly line slid easily through the guides in the approximate direction of the last green shadow. I could see its bright member lying straight to the spot. Stripping slowly, I felt it tighten as though it had hung up on something, fully conscious that there was nothing on this clean bottom that could do that sort of thing but a bass. He flailed the quiet surface once, took most of the flyline against the drag, then surrendered in the shallows. Then I repeated the process until I had four on the beach and then tucked them away just before a set of headlights rounded the Race curve.

The New Yorker killed his headlights before they had a chance to glow upon the bar. Then he shut down and walked casually down to the edge 200 feet to my right. The lighthouse only had to glow in his forefront a couple of times before he went to his buggy for different gear. He knew. I hooked up for a few seconds, long enough to get his attention, then dropped the fish. Then, he splashed over to me to ask if I had taken any of the "ton" of bass that were about. Telling him that I hadn't, he shuffled off saying something about picky fish. I know that fishing with the flyrod made him uneasy because he suspected that it might work and if it did he would be S.O.L. because who has a flyrod when striper fishing? By the time I beached my third in front of him, he was growling:

"I wouldn't a believed it if I didn't see it with me own eyes."

Such episodes with the eel-fly were not uncommon as the thing had an incredible capacity for putting stripers off their guard. It was part of the family.

Those first days with the Rapala were the beginning of a lifelong encounter with a whole *genre* of striper plugs, which really originated in Finland with Laure Rapala. Seeing that he had a killer, a number of American manufacturers came out with a version of their own that was competitive in effectiveness. Plug makers were imitating each other at such a rate that some ended up in court. But from a fishing viewpoint, I would say that the Rebel dominated the market; it certainly dominated our equipment.

When the fish were small, we used the 5½ inch floater, tied direct to the mono, with no wire leader or snap. Conditions depending, we often relied upon the one ounce, 7 inch floater model; and, around that time in the early 70's, there was a "Wind Cheater Super Minnow" that was six inches long that has the best casting qualities of them all. Moreover, it weighed 1¼ ounces and still floated—a quality that was needed to deal with stripers that were feeding upon sand eels.

With Dickie well into his teens, he learned just about everything I did and the flyrod and eel-fly were no exception. Moreover, the lad was enjoying his first position of power in life: He knew how to tie flies and would spend hours during daylight winding the six white feathers of saddle hackle to a 2/0 stainless hook. Together we had some serious fishing while flycasting

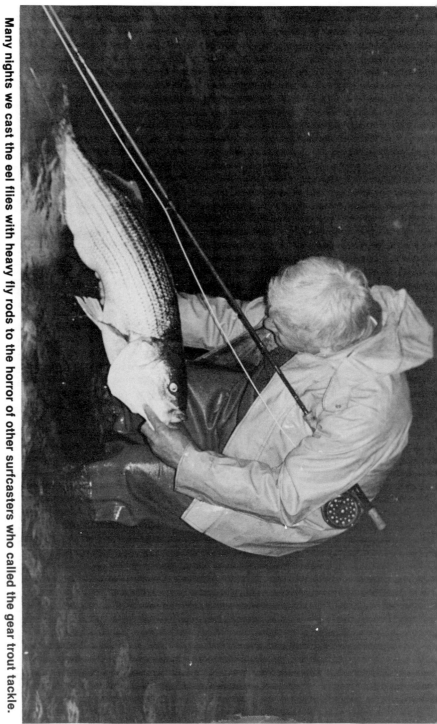

Many nights we cast the eel flies with heavy fly rods to the horror of other surfcasters who called the gear trout tackle.

the shore of the Race. Usually, we did this in a moderate onshore wind, say, 10 to 20 knots. But the failing of the flyrod was that its best application came during conditions that were identical to those we used while fishing Rebels. We often agonized over whether to fly fish or spin cast the Rebels, the debate raging on about efficiency, distance, lure costs and bass prices.

We had seen droppers used back at Nauset in the beginning. Some used bucktail streamers and others would lash a small strip of pork rind to a hook. Both lacked sophistication though they at times did account for impressive takes of bass. Our eel-fly, however, had proven itself without the influence of a large striper plug. And we were planning to tow the fly with the finest striper plugs made. Two killers!

With a wind, and that was most of the time, we could come up with a total take that was greater than either the plug or fly would catch independently. In addition, the teaser system, which was a three foot leader with an eight inch section that fell from the swivel, could be used by Mom and all the girls. No longer a case of choosing whether to use the fly or plug, we let the stripers do it. The Rebel and eel-fly had one failing: the plug was not the best thing for casting.

Nights when the sou'west was clipping over 30 knots, sending foam sliding behind us, waves six feet, the Rebels didn't cut it. I had a number of Gibbs Swimmers, which were fondly known by the gang as "bottle plugs." These are hand fashioned wooden creations that neck down thin below the head which has a weird swimmer plate cut right out of the body. I don't like to tamper with anybody's religion because I know that one man's junk is another's killer when it comes to striper fishing, but this is my book and I have to tell you ... that bottle plug is the worst fish catcher ever made. That thing couldn't catch a fish in a hatchery where the attendants had been on vacation for a week. But oh boy does it ever cast! Nights, when seamen hoisted gale warning flags at the Coast Guard Station, we skimmed those rocket shaped bottle plugs over the wave tops to do a job. How good, or, how bad? Once, during a string of consecutive 30 knot nights, we landed 103 stripers with the bottle plug and eel fly combo; 102 took the fly.

There are bound to be nights, even if it is only twice per year, when the sou'west will howl at a steady 50 and gust to ten knots over that. Nights like these the trawlers fight to keep the bow into the sea for their lives. Sport fishermen move to the lee of Cape Cod if they are going to fish at all; and, if you park your buggy in the wrong place, the wind will take the paint off and frost your windshield permanently. When a surfcaster faces such a tempest he turns his face to breathe, wears a foul weather top to keep his body dry from the wave tops blowing across him, and casts low barely clear of wave crests. Then, he reels up line while the plug bobs ineffectively behind him.

But when the sou'west has pushed all that warm, nutrient rich, surface water against the beach, bait feasting upon the plankton, bass and blues gorging upon that bait, who wants to wait in the wings for it to subside? When you have had their number night after night, and you have spent half your life finding out what makes them vulnerable, *knowing* that they are there, would you allow yourself to be counted out by the very conditions for which you prayed?

We had that kind of wind building on an August day after nearly a week of winds that we handled with bottle plugs. The girls had spent the day in the buggy because the sand was stinging their legs. By mid-afternoon the truck wheels were sitting on four mounds and though there was sun, the surface of the beach, for a height of 10 feet, had a smoky pall of suspended sand and water lashing at everything in its path. The boy was rigging bottles when I told him to stow them, that we would be casting five ounce bank sinkers that night. Then, when the tide was down four hours, close to 2:00 A.M., we casted the woefully small flies—towed by sinkers—into the maelstrom and caught stripers as though Race Point was their chosen place to die.

The dock was quiet the next day when Dick and I made our two box drop because what few trawlers that had been out had apparently cut their trips short from the heavy seas. And there were no fish brought in by the beach people. One of the boat captains was sitting in the office like he owned the place—big guy, high forties, black mustache, Portuguese accent, smoking a stogie. Working around him, I wrote up the fish, then rummaged through the stack of beach checks for ours. It was a decent payoff that I had already seen but had left there to grind the agates of the gang that would see it when picking up their own.

Shoving it in his face, I asked, "Hey Cappy, how's that for fishin' the beach a week?"

Looking at the bottom line of $590, his face went a little flush, perhaps thinking about his investment sitting idle at the dock straining its lines.

"Kid," he said, "there's a lot of weeks, after the bank, inn-surance, and a crew, when I don't make that." Then he blew some acrid smoke toward the ceiling and stared blankly at its swirls.

CHAPTER 9

Wolf at the Door

By 1974 the war babies were looking down the barrel of 30 years old. Also coming of age were the heretofore unknown population levels of stripers from the Chesapeake where each year produced a young of the year index that dwarfed what is born today; allow me to explain.

For about 35 years the Maryland Department of Natural Resources has surveyed 40 different sites around Chesapeake Bay to determine the number of young of the year bass. The number of such juvenile fish netted—stripers per haul—has enabled officials to establish an index which is a measurement of spawning success. An index of 10 is considered an average year and those of the sixties were nearly all above that; moreover, the index peaked at 30.4 fish per netting in 1970.

To us, stripers were everywhere as we drew from those burgeoning year classes. But there was difference of opinion as to the future of striper fishing. Many conservationists preached that an end was near for stripers. Bob Pond, who was the inventor of some of our finest striper plugs and founder of Stripers Unlimited, spoke before clubs all along the striper coast warning of a loss of viability in this fine gamefish. Some believed him and came forward with both moral and financial support for his continued work. However, some of us, with the sight of great schools of linesides fresh in our minds, felt that there was too much empirical evidence to the contrary for Pond to be believable. I always had the greatest respect for Bob as a man and surfcaster who had taught me something of how to fish for bass back in Westport when I was but a rough cut stone. Politely, he, and many other of his ilk, were wrong.

Born out of a love-starved population boom that followed WWII, the yuppies were causing the Cape to sink from the weight of their beach buggies and boat trailers. It was no secret that the money it cost in gasoline, depth finders and fishing tackle was retrievable, to some degree, in husky fish checks at the dock. Where there had been a small gaggle of buggies in years past, the vast stretches of emptiness between were filling with expensive, camper equipped four wheel pickups. The selectmen of Orleans and Chatham had seen it first in '70 when they imposed the three day rule. Coupled with Nauset's overflow, P-Town's National Seashore Park had doubled in fishing rigs. Officials tightened the screws.

First they changed the name of our homes to "Self-Contained-Vehicles"; then they established Self-Contained-Vehicle areas which were designated with signs that detracted from the esthetics of the beach. They imposed fees which nobody cared about. They abolished the Race Point Area and one to the east on the Back Beach, crowding more of us into double lines where, on weekends, we often found ourselves parked two feet apart. Speed limits, permit checks, loaded guns. Then, the thing that we had feared the most—a 21 day per season regulation.

Spoon-fed in small doses, the fishermen of Cape Cod each year watched more of their freedoms deprived from them without their uttering a modicum of objection. Had the imposition of such impossible regulation been brought to bear at one time, there would have been riotous resistance. But the government men are too smart for that. For them it begins with a hand upon the knee. Much in the way they romanced their girl friends as

Huge catches of stripers came in from all over the Cape. But, as fishing got better the Rangers started tightening the screws.

school boys, they "managed" fishermen from their beach, with the same results. So much for maintaining the local culture.

For once our arithmetic was without pounds and dollars. There were ten weeks to our summers. The Park Service didn't begin their 21 day count until July 1st, which meant that there were really only eight weeks to worry about. If we used three days per week and went to Nauset Beach for three, we could chisel a couple of hours at each end that would somehow come out to seven days. With such a day shuffle, we had seven weeks out of eight covered.

With six of us fishing full time we could make the best boat fishermen look like amateurs. It isn't that we were that good, and the kids—particularly the girls—only fished when the bass were practically under the buggy, but we had a system that monitored the fishing at both Race Point and Chatham Inlet, only the finest striper water in the world. Fish checks had begun to attract attention at the dock once we left the bluefishing of the first year. I blame the wholesaler.

After unloading the boxes, you separate the bass and blues, weigh them up yourself, then write up the slip with your name, date, species and poundage. There are two carbons and you keep the bottom one, the pink. The others go into an open basket on the desk with all the other drops of fish. In a closed drawer is last week's check with all the drops for that week stapled on. Depending upon when you pick up the check, anybody can have a running account of how much fish you caught the previous week and, on a daily basis, what you've been dropping. Fine, if the accountant empties the basket regularly. But this guy was overworked and you could sometimes peruse through the basket and see who dropped what for the last three days. It was a great way for me to keep tabs on the others, have a relative measurement of our success. But, they were doing the same thing and four, five and six hundred dollar, choke-a-horse payoffs for a surfcaster attract no small measure of attention.

When we disappeared for three days during the week nobody knew where we were and I know now that the payoffs at the dock caused considerable speculation about this. It was widely known that we were fond of the Race, but if any amount of detective work was done, it could be quickly determined that we had not been there. Moreover, in those occasional conversations that sometimes come up at the dock or while pumping gas, I would mention far away places that were not producing like the Canal, Sandy Neck, or Rhode Island. It threw some people off, or maybe slowed them down. Any time we had a bad trip at Nauset, I would instruct the children to make frequent mention to their friends of how pleasant it was to be home for a few days and take hot showers. While gone, we could have been anywhere.

For the first time life on Cape Cod had gotten complicated. It had gotten so to the degree that a number of ponderable problems needed both understanding and workable solutions. I cannot recall, at this relatively early age, feeling the burden both of guilt and pressing need to go on at the same time. At heart, I was a sport fisherman. Yet, I was taking and marketing a fish that was in demand. It helped me to feel better about this when I thought about the millions of pounds netted and trapped, many on their way to their very natal rivers. I assumed that the power, the government, a greater force than one man, some ill defined wisdom more potent than I, would have long ago stopped our killing of the fish if it was so wrong that the eco-system could not endure it.

It seemed that everywhere I turned I flew in the face of all that I had once

For the first time life on Cape Cod had gotten complicated. It had gotten to the degree that a number of ponderable problems needed both understanding and workable solutions.

held dear in terms of how one is supposed to behave in an ordered society. Lying? Failure to tell the truth about what does, where one goes—so *gauche*! I remember the posters at Summer Street School in the North End where a little girl, who looked so much like Jane, the character of early readers, said that the policeman is our friend. My brother was a policeman. Worse, I'm a teacher, duty bound to set examples, not just to children, but to those around who remained that respected the profession. Still, I had come to despise the Park Police, the regulations, the constraints, the loss of freedom. On one hand I understand why all this was coming about; on the other, there was a side of me that rebelled. Agonizing over the long term implications of the three—fish, my friends, social order—I often fretted over what striper fishing was doing to me. At times the enigma paralyzed my sense of logic. How does one separate rationalization of one's behavior from what he feels is right?

It was perhaps over rationalized, but it was done because perhaps we had been there too long. The life continued because, for the first time, we had our independence and had begun to profit from it.

It started with people having a good time with the bluefish. The real action was coming.

CHAPTER 10

Action at Pochet Hole

Switching beaches twice a week was not a relaxing way to spend the summer but it dealt with all our problems nicely, as well as raised our poundages at the dock. We nearly always caught more stripers at Nauset which prevented us from much rest while surfcasting there. Moreover, because of our stretch of the clock, we usually fished it for 3½ nights, coming off late to a sleepy, unsuspecting guard at the check point who could care less what we did. Then, between airing up and gas, as well as the drive north, it would be around 4:00 A.M. by the time we pulled up to the dock to unload. Here, we grabbed a few hours before the dockmaster was out of the sheets. That rare occasion when we had no fish, we slept at Beech Forest, which is one of those nature walk places the Park Service maintained for tourists. Then, Joyce would stagger through the aisles of the A&P for supplies, grabbing a bunch of cooked chickens and Arturo's bread which we ate in the parking lot to kill time until the ranger station opened at 9:00. It was a grueling routine that a surfcaster who spent all his nights greeting the sunrise could live without.

This particular trip, nobody had even the sniff of a striper the full length of Nauset so we drove past Pochet mid-afternoon Sunday, actually *early* in the spending of our precious 72 hours. Nearest to the beach access point, there was a healthy spread of tourists and townies playing with beach balls and lying on blankets. Among them was a small gallery of people in swim suits gathered around a caster who was fighting a bluefish. Each time the thing leaped, the caster bowed his rod tip in an exaggerated way to the delight and admiration of his audience who dutifully applauded either the bluefish, the fisherman, or both. It was all sort of amateurish, but kind of interesting to watch. We shut the truck down.

Viewing the whole thing with condescension, I thought about all the years that we had passed Pochet Hole without ever seeing anything in the way of gamefish action. It is one of those places where you wouldn't want to hit them for fear of wasting time for years after. Still, in all fairness to the spot, it had a lot of class. Miles of Nauset have an outer bar, but here, the bar edges seaward as if to go around a deep, green hole, indicating by its shading a far greater depth than one can find anywhere else along the beach. The opening is distinctive in its appearance because of the white foam that breaks upon the bars flanking it.

I soon grew tired of watching the fellow fighting the fish and focused elsewhere. Then, I noticed a black shoal of baitfish moving at the south end that changed shape rapidly. Eyes training upon other parts of the hole, there was a line of the same color near the surf that flashed a trifle of silver. Another bluefish cartwheeled deep in the hole. Unless you can take a ton when nobody else can, there's no money in bluefish. Still, I had a gnawing, back-of-the-mind feeling that Pochet should be viewed with greater scrutiny.

Rigging a wire and popper, I splashed out onto the north finger of bar to look around. The popper drew no takers, but I was enjoying the coolness of the daylight surf on my jeans, watching with polaroids. Then a dark shadow, four feet long, slid over the bar not three yards from me. I waded deeper. Then a pair of dark green forms of similar size lazed slowly away from me.

My God!

Trying to seem nonchalant, I walked as quickly as I dared back to the buggy. Inside, I told Joyce and the kids what we had in front of us while Dick and I donned waders and parkas and belted down. Whether it was a cloud, or lower sun, the light had changed enough to betray huge schools of blueback herring milling about in the hole. Dick was bending 7 inch Rebels direct to the mono of all the rods, then he shoved a spare into his parka and handed me another.

When an area has 11 foot tides, mid tide the water rises quickly. Even in the few short minutes that I had been gone, enough water had come up to prevent me from going as far out on the bar as I had been. In spite of this the green shadows of huge stripers were still there and I gasped at every one, poor Dickie unable to see a one without the sunglasses. There had been one brief follow on my swimmer when I passed the polaroids to the boy who held them against his face and gasped. There was nothing under 25 pounds!

Behind us huge shoals of bluebacks discolored the bowl to gray. For all but the 200 foot wide opening on the seaward side, the bait was confined within the bars that encircled them. It seemed as if they knew that certain death waited for them on the outside. As the tide rose, pushing at us, it was the most astounding sight of our fishing lives. I've seen them hundreds of times before, busting or rolling or twisting their bodies through the surf after bait. But never, until that day, had I stood among them to watch them cruise by like pets. First, one long, dark form; then three; and then we gasped as a save of fish passed so close that the motion of a shaky, backlashed cast flushed them out of sight. These were not the small fish that we so often caught.

An intimacy develops out of a lifetime of mid-watch hunts for stripers where you think you know something about them. For the hundreds, if not thousands, of stripers I have taken, there have been so few times when you could see one in the brightness of the sun; and catching one was even more rare. These brutes seemed to exhibit a certain organization in their behavior. It made me wonder if this was the way they always acted and I was seeing it for the first time; or, was it some scheme that they had put into play to herd the herring into the hole and keep them there. Yes, a few pods of herring took a pasting well into the hole, though we could not tell if the frothy bursts were made by bass or the renegade bluefish. What we could see most vividly were the patrols of thugs passing back and forth on the bar as if guarding the cache, the trap comprised of sand and sea. Yet, some fish would scurry over the bar, as if their turn to kill had come. Meanwhile the assigned guards never broke ranks from the bar we fished from, showing little interest in our plugs. Our frustrations mounted, seeing so many great bass and being unable to interest them. We would see a cow on the left, cast, hearts skipping a beat, the monster would trail the plug for a few yards then turn away. Or, we picked a larger group and had even poorer results.

It was not until we cast blindly into the hole—a feat requiring considerable resignation—that we felt the throb of a take. Here, it seemed, the ones that were feasting engulfed the plugs with an abandon that eclipsed the cautiousness of those on the bar. Dick's drag groaned under the force of a striper that hightailed out over the bar, a wave lifting him off his feet. As I shouted encouragement, my rod tip was hauled down into the surf from the force of a strike. We traded positions and passed lines over one another, fighting the rising surf as we inched our way back to shallower water.

Apparently, and I'll never quite be sure of this, those stripers that we could see, could see us. When we turned to blind casting, we benefited from the cover of distance. There may have been more stripers in the hole.

A few casters without waders joined us but they had ineffectual poppers and also soon grew numb from the cold surf. Dickie was dragging our pair of 30 pounders to the dry beach when I hooked up again. When he rejoined me, he urged that we head back to the buggy with Mom and the girls because everybody was casting furiously by then. It was plain, judging from the line of people on the shore, that all hell had broken loose. Mom and the girls were good, but they weren't that good. We ran.

Anglers were spread for 300 feet in a pandemonium of monofilament, bare feet, and careless surfrods, lashing in all directions, while the bluebacks took a whipping in the first wave from what few could see, it seemed, the largest stripers we had ever encountered. Hungrily, the linesides tore through the first wave while the picnickers hurled their poppers as far as they could. There wasn't a swimming plug in the line, except those that the girls were throwing and they had found their mark.

Both the twins backed up the beach as their spinning rods arched. In my foreshore a covey of herring darted into the air while a bass, easily a foot longer than anything we had seen, lanced at them just below a wave crest. I was in the midst of giving Sandra help with the gaff when I turned in time to see a bather go down to help Susan with her fish. Just as the lineside was in the first wave, he grabbed the line in an effort to help her and it broke.

When I hauled Sandra's fish up onto the beach, one around 20 pounds, I noticed pennants of mono hanging from her plug. Certain that it was no knot of Dickie's, I asked about it.

"I had to tie the plug on," she said, "I lost the other when a man tried to help me."

However well meaning these people might have been, it was a certainty that these 11 year old girls knew more about dealing with a wild fish in the surf than they did. But that is the price of having their mentor away.

Then I tied another swimmer to Susan's line, gaffed a large bass for a fellow beside me, and heard the report of parting mono ten yards to my right just before a fellow hurled his surfrod onto the sand. Mom was dragging a cow toward the truck for Carol, and Dickie hunched over his squidder while his drag washers heated from the run of a good fish.

Seizing upon a clear moment when nobody seemed to need help, I turned with my rod in time to see the same, five foot behemoth dart briefly through the surf again. It had to be a striper that challenged the World Record; and it had to be the same one I had viewed earlier. Certainly, there were not *two* such fish in our surf. Having already killed one that later weighed 43 pounds, the one I was seeing was twice that size!

More bluebacks sprinkled hell west and big fish came up again while my rod was cocked for the next cast. The take was instantaneous, but to my astonishment, I hooked a much smaller fish in the thirties which never gained its head as I backed violently in time with a breaking wave. The green bass bounced on the dry sand while I spiked the rod on the truck. A stranger beside me called, asking what he was doing wrong, and I threw him a swimmer which I never saw again.

Dick was boxing fish feverishly to get them out of sight in advance of a pair of campers coming down the beach. On the dry shore there were only two stripers which had rolled enough sand on them to make them invisible. What was apparent were the bluefish that were lying everywhere, a direct result of all the poppers in use. Because of this, the campers passed without ever slowing just as the weekend rigs, numbering at least 50, had done earlier. With the sun lowering, the beach people had thinned down to a mere handful, victims, I'm sure, of the weariness of the day and the frustration of having so many uncooperative bass in front of them.

Carol and the twins were still doing a job when Mom and Dickie spiked their sticks to help them. I saw the big bass again, this time 25 yards to the left. Running to where I guessed he was, I waited, saw him roll in the white suds, layed a short cast just past him, and felt the take and surge as he seized

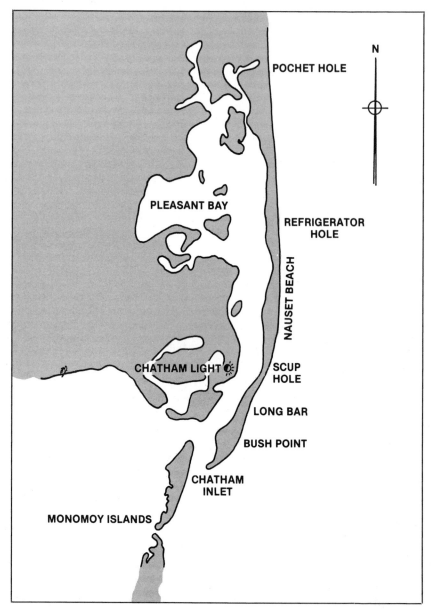

N

POCHET HOLE

PLEASANT BAY

REFRIGERATOR HOLE

NAUSET BEACH

CHATHAM LIGHT

SCUP HOLE

LONG BAR

BUSH POINT

CHATHAM INLET

MONOMOY ISLANDS

the plug then headed seaward. The 45 pound braid tumbled from the spool, seeming to melt away quickly to dry portions of the line deep in the reel. Cracking the star open, I tried to guess how far he had gone and when he would tire to sulk deep. Well past the outer bar, I saw what had to be him flail the surface. Then, with no more than 20 yards of line left, I sickened at the realization that he had somehow shaken the plug. So much for World Records.

Much to the satisfaction of us all, it was sunset before the smoke of Pochet cleared. The large cooler on the front bumper held only nine of the 27 linesides that we had taken—over 600 pounds. In the aisle of our living quarters the 30 pounders made movement in the truck difficult. As it turned out, we had a pretty good load.

While Mom put a dinner together, Dick and I watched for holdouts that might have stayed in the hole but the falling tide apparently influenced the bait and there was nothing. Late that night we went through the check point, drove north to P-Town, the children singing nearly the full distance, and went on the beach there without a permit to sleep. Next morning we were off before the Ranger Station opened.

We would have liked to stop and have them charge us for the day (just kidding) but we wanted to make the dock before there was too much activity and before the sun went to work on the fish. There we topped off with ice and headed south back to Nauset.

Never having checked on there that early in the day, I was certain that the guard would not recognize us to note that we had not been gone for 72 hours. However, my concern was that if anybody checked the beach log our permit number would show up too soon bringing attention to the fact. If we could change permit numbers we would be clean. If we were caught changing numbers we wouldn't. Worse, what if the number we gave belonged to someone else who was either on the beach during the last 72 hours or was going on during the next three days? Of course, a child can make a mistake.

At the check point Sandra ran to the guard shack, calling, "476, six on board."

The guard, looking up from his paperback, responded politely, "Thank you, little lady."

Grinning at our P-Town permit, 476, Sandra hopped into the camper, and slammed the door to signal that we could drive on.

When we arrived at Pochet there were no other fishermen, the beach desolate, the tide low, and not a shred of evidence of what had happened the day before could be found. The kids all took their dip in the surf and I crawled up to the top bunk, pulled a bag to my chin, and permitted a friendly wind to blow the fragrances of Pleasant Bay into my dreams.

The knock on the door by the Chatham police officer came late enough to minimize any disturbance he might have caused.

"Sorry to bother you, Sir," his manner artificially polite, "but I was wondering when you came on."

"Roughly late morning, maybe eleven," I responded, trying to sound as matter of fact as I could.

"Sir, we have a complaint that you left the beach sometime yesterday and failed to absent yourself the required time."

"Sir," with the same artificial, exaggerated and strained courtesy, "you folks spend over thirty thousand a year to assure that nobody stays on 73 hours, you could check the book instead of waking a tired surfcaster to ask something that you already know."

His irritation difficult to hide, the officer told me that he would and drove off.

A half hour later he was back saying that there were no irregularities. Now that I was awake, I recognized that I had handled him badly and tried to be a little more polite, offering him coffee, even a beer, if he was about to go off duty. We engaged in pleasant conversation as he slid into the cab of his vehicle. Then, he took his cap off, as if he was about to speak in a more off the cuff manner:

"Frank," he said, "I know who you are and what you are trying to do. If somebody saw you, they saw you. I'm not going ..."

"Listen," I interrupted, horrified at the thought that I was about to become beholding to one of these guys, "if you've got a case, I want to see a signed complaint. I have a right to know my accuser. It's part of my defense."

At that moment, it was more important to me to know who was gaffing me than whether or not I was making another mistake. Lucky for me that the officer didn't want to press it. Instead he seemed mildly irritated, as though he knew that he could do me in and didn't want to. He killed his ignition, kind of slouched back in his seat, with a long breath and layed it all out.

"Look Frank, we're not out to get anybody. It's a question of people being indiscreet, creating heat. If we have a complaint we have to check it out. I got a complaint and I saw your truck over the weekend at the inlet ..."

"Who?"

"That doesn't matter, but ..."

"Who?"

"Just be a little more careful. Know who your friends are."

"I want to know who my enemies are. I want to know what bastard fishes with me one night and then makes up stories about me later."

Seeming amused at my tenacity over my innocence, he started his pickup, grinning at my heightened irritation, fully knowing that it was more important for me to know *who* had done this than dealing with its consequences. Then, he seemed to break down with his game as though he felt sorry for me. Violating the cardinal, all-abiding rule of law enforcement, he fused a situation by describing my accuser in detail. I then knew precisely who it was.

Joyce began to cry when I told her what a friend at Nauset for eight years had done to us. But it didn't surprise me that he was a member of our own striper club. I was beginning to recognize that success had its own price; I was seeing that more and more people resented our freedom. We had our love, our youth, our health. We wandered Cape Cod at will without regard for those who would try to stop us. We would continue to catch striped bass until the last day or last striper and there was nobody that was going to stop us.

Dickie came in dripping sea water and wearing polaroids to report that not a solitary blueback could be found in the hole. He didn't have to be sent on such a mission, because the boy was now tidewise enough to remember yesterday's conditions and watch for them. I should have known that you couldn't trust that Pochet Hole. The place was just a flash in the pan, nothing more.

We waited until dark, until the Ranger Station in P-Town would be closed so that they wouldn't charge us for a day, made a few half-hearted casts to be certain that no stripers were cruising after dark to look for yesterday's goodies, and left.

At the check point Sandra dutifully yelled "476" to the guard, then scurried into the camper.

Just as the clutch left the floorboard he called, "Wait a minute." And we left, pretending not to hear.

CHAPTER 11

Sleights of Hand

The complications had crept up on us so slowly over the five years since the regulations had tightened up at Nauset, that it had taken that long for us to realize we had lost our flexibility. In theory, the striper activity was supposed to dictate our fishing. But it had become far from that. Instead, we found ourselves staying a little longer here, or leaving a little early for there, because it was a way of dealing with the two edged sword of three days per week at Nauset or 21 days per season in P-Town.

It was pretty tough to beat Nauset because the place was guarded around the clock like a landfill. But the Cape Cod National Seashore was being beat all the time.

There was no more money involved after you bought your annual permit. After that each time that you went on the beach they issued you an overnight pass for up to three days, which was charged to your record for the season until you had used up your 21 days. The pass was a 5"x 9" file card that had been run through a mimeograph machine with the hand lettered words "Cape Cod National Seashore (centered) Self-Contained Vehicle Permit." Type written at the bottom was a blank line for your permit number and a line for the ranger to sign it. What they did to turn the blank form into an active permit was scroll a large number of your expiration date with a magic marker, date stamp it, and then sign it. For instance, if it was issued on the 3rd for three days, they would write a big 6 with the magic marker.

Their system was flawed because they didn't ever require the return of the old permits. Thus, everybody in Race City kept their old passes, knowing that the July pass with a six on it could be displayed in the window of the buggy in August any time between the third and sixth. Moreover, if you had a black magic marker, you could add a one or two in front of the six either of the months. But the geniuses at the Ranger Station must have caught on to that because within a year they were issuing permits that were numbered with red, green, and blue. This caused everybody to go out and get the color kits, but it did take some doing to make a green six into a black 16.

Naturally, after a couple of years of this, most people had quite a store, a variety pack, if you will, of varied numbers in various colors, but always with higher numbers, which enabled them to snitch enough extra days to get them through a summer of weekends along with a two week vacation. We were fishing full time, and the system of phoney permits was both uneasy, when they led somebody off the beach and stressy, when the ranger took the trouble to get out of his jeep to examine yours more closely. Sometimes I think that it was all a game and that they knew what everybody was doing. With our particular problems we needed something better.

One night, while coming back late from Nauset, it occurred to me to rip the hasp off the lock at the Ranger Station and grab a million blank passes; but that would have been breaking and entering. Another time that double dippin' sonofabitch, a retired Chief Boatswain Mate of 30 years now working as a ranger, was writing us a legal pass when the phone rang.

"Ranger Station," as he lifted the phone with his back to me and a stack of blank permits. Reaching for the stack, my fingers closed upon a half-inch of them. But just as I started to lift them, he turned, and I had to swat the pile saying, "Friggin horseflies, I hate um." God, if he had given me just a

There were a lot of nights when we ached for a bluefish when stripers were nowhere to be found.

few more seconds.

Sometimes, in the afternoon when the sou'west blew through the screen of the top bunk, I would fantasize about what it would be like to get a bunch of those blank passes. Once, I realized that our tow cable was too thick to fit through the padlock and I planned to attach a smaller cable to it and rip it out with the truck. It could have been done in two-wheel drive. Then, in a masterful stroke of ingenuity, the idea came to me: Print the blank passes ourselves! Brilliant.

First, I layed some cheap bond on the pass and traced the wording; then, once the wording was finished, I lined up a blank 5x9 card, a sheet of black carbon paper and my thin bond, holding them together with a pair of paper clips. Then I simply retraced the wording. That first time, those long moments when my now larcenous mind contemplated the result, seemed an eternity rewarded with an intense feeling of accomplishment. Once the typing was on at the bottom, printed with the same carbon paper, my passes were as nice as those they issued. It became a joke with Joyce and me that the one way we might get caught was that our passes were better than those the Park Service used. These blanks had to be made one at a time as I was not equipped to go into full production at the beach. For the ranger's signature, we just scribbled something that was illegible because at the Ranger Station they were used to that.

The first thing any serious surfcaster did when outfitting a buggy was rig a fish box on the front bumper. Fish could be stored and transported to the dock without interfering with or fouling the living quarters. Moreover, its forward position helped in the vehicle's weight distribution.

The real test in a Cape surfcaster's ability to manage his life properly was how he handled that box. Dare brag about a good catch too soon after it happened and the guy you told would tell his friends who would tell their friends. How fast the news traveled was proportionate to how fresh the news was; and, certainly if you dispelled all doubt by lifting the cover and showing fish so fresh that you hadn't had time to bring them to the dock yet, a modest 300 pound load would be a half ton by sunset. You might be the hero of the Cape Cod closed society of surfcasters today but you sure are not going to be alone tonight.

The trap of this situation is that once you show somebody the truth, you have to keep telling the truth. Naturally, anybody that sees a good catch of fish is going to want to know where and when they were taken. Many stupid people that I have known think that they can have it at both ends by bragging about their success then lying about where it was done. There is no quicker way to destroy yourself socially. Nothing angers a fisherman more than a wild goose chase. I didn't mind being unpopular, but I didn't want to be hated. And if they are angry they will never forget what is done to them, nor who did it. For the rest of your fishing life they will wait for the chance to steer you wrong and getting you will become as big a sport, as compelling an endeavor, as surfcasting itself.

Deciding who should be told about the fishing was so complicated, so entangled with who was whose friend that we simply let it be known that we were not talking about fish with anybody. I was tired of being flogged by weekenders who couldn't keep their mouths shut. Naturally, it didn't take long for many of the beach regulars that I had known for many years to shun us when for years there had always been a friendly wave. I truly wish that I could have been more insensitive to the feelings of others toward us, but the loss of the most distant friend has always seemed to me to be a bitter price for being a rod and reel commercial.

You might be the hero of the Cape Cod closed society of surfcasters today but you are not going to be alone tonight.

From our earliest days as greenhorns back at Nauset we had been cheated by others repeatedly. Not all of them, but with many the attitudes were of the here and now. They would sweet talk you and back slap you to get all they could then tell their friends the things they knew were in the strictest of confidence. There were always enough guys around who were ready to trade manure for oats, saying something about some made up blitz somewhere then wait for you to tell them something they could use. They must have thought that such bad trades would slip from my memory. Never forget that I spent more time in the Cape Cod striper surf in one season than many regulars there spent in a lifetime. And that experience had taught me plenty of what games people played. Fishing full time, we were always in tune with the situation, knowing exactly where bass were being taken on a regular basis. If the going thing went sour, we would explore the beach, at various stages of tide, until we discovered something new. If we wanted to pay some bills we had to work. We talk here about blitz and boxes of fish and choke-a-horse folding green but there were hundreds of nights when our hands ached for nothing—not even a 15 cent bluefish. Then, along come these weekenders, knowing nothing, owing everybody a favor, expecting us to lay it all out for them.

Curiously, my New York comrades seemed to admire my silence. This gave me the feeling that it was they who understood my situation most. As a young bumpkin from Massachusetts, how could I guess that an idle conversation with me told them more about the fishing than if they had asked? It was Pat Abate, a writer, surfcaster, and occasional visitor to our buggy for generalized beach palaver, that clued me in on the realities. I quote him as best I can from memory:

"Frank, these guys don't have to ask you about the fishing. They see it in your manner. It takes only a couple of minutes with you to tell how good the fishing is because when you are taking fish you swagger and you act like you're speeding your brains out. Everybody knows that there is only one thing that can make you that way. It is a joke with them."

Several more things can be said about my new-found "company policy" —a term I layed on it because it appealed to the industrial minds. Soon after it became widely known that I wasn't talking fishing anymore, one of the regulars, who had quit his job in the city, stopped me in the track coming from the dock one day to congratulate me on my silence, saying that he understood and that we full timers had to stick together on this, that he too was tired of bird dogging stripers for all them tourists. The implications of the way he spoke to me were that he was exempt from the policy. Late that summer Joe Crowe, another commercial who had always kept to himself but had somehow managed to communicate a mutuality, a comradeship, dropped by one night to whisper that they had been doing a job at Highland Light. Pressing his open palms in front of him and backing, he said, "You don't owe me for this. I know how you feel." Shaking his head nervously as though he wanted to pass the word on and get away as quickly as possible, he jumped back into his buggy, his voice trailing off, saying something about seeing us down there. It had become a case of the best fishermen, who know the most, always willing to come forward, feeling it seemed that no blitz should ever come off without Frank Daignault.

Yet, whenever we hit the fish on our own we kept it quiet and none of the real die-hards seemed ever to take it personally. It was as though they completely understood, that it was an impersonal thing, a thing that had to be done in the name of harmony in the beach community.

But the box was the one thing that could betray me, and it did, at least un-

Deciding who should be told about fishing was so complicated, so entangled, we simply decided not to talk fish with anybody.

til I learned to use it. Most mornings we were in bed by sunrise, but there were always people of Race City standing around with the dawn: the boatmen, or slackers who had slept the night, chatting about fishing, practicing their jargon. This particular day I felt a vibration in the camper, a movement, that by itself wouldn't have awakened me were it not for all the exclamations close to the front bumper. Can you imagine the balls of a guy opening your fish box to see what was in it! Worse, the fishing was believed to be poor that year, late July, with most of the crowd waiting for the bluefish run to start and we had five or six stripers over 30 pounds packed. Not a large catch by the standards of the time, but for those who *thought* that fishing was bad, who didn't catch that many bass in a season, the revelation touched off a small riot in Race City. From then on there was a lock on the fish box.

Of course the outrageous effect of keeping a lock on the box was not a message that we feared having our fish stolen. Rather, it was a clear message that its contents was classified information and the implications, even when it was empty, were that it was full.

My next exercise in *legerdemain* was to get those fish slips that sat at the dock out of full view of every grunting, sniffing interloper. What with all the years, I had been doing business longer with the dock than the accountant, Kenny, who worked there. One afternoon I dropped by and layed my case before him pointing out that a person's fish check was a sensitive matter that was too important to endure the perusal of just anybody. He agreed to keep it in the office. Then, without making as big a case out of it, I later started bringing my daily fish slips up to him with a friendly wink. Kenny turned out to be one of the nicest townies that I ever got to know on the Cape; maybe he came from somewhere else.

There was a certain vicarious satisfaction in dropping a load of fish and then walking upstairs to deliver the drop slip. It had set me apart from the other fishermen of the beach who enjoyed having their occasional successes made public. Many Saturday mornings, when I climbed the stairs to the, ahem, "Main Office" everyone seemed to wonder where I was going. And I, basking in the one-upmanship of being now among the trawler skippers who delivered their fish by the ton, felt like a real torpedo. But, like the box, I had introduced a measure of mystery in the minds of some; with others, the absence of a check for them to leer over implied we weren't catching any fish; and, still others assumed the checks were too big to be on the desk.

Dave Docwra, United Kingdom distance casting champion, readies a cast which could go up to 700 feet!

CHAPTER 12

The Caster

Spring of 1975, I got a letter from Frank Woolner, who was both my editor and mentor in the writing game. Then, I had been writing about surf fishing for five years in *Salt Water Sportsman* magazine and Frank, who had taken me under his wing, had an unusual assignment for me. He wanted me to take Dave Docwra, who was the United Kingdom distance casting champion, surf fishing on the Cape.

From what I pieced together, Docwra would have liked to have his hand at the World Championships, but his government would not finance his trip to South Africa for a go at them and the Australians. Apparently his trip to the U.S. was some sort of protest response to the dispute which was further supported by his real love of surfcasting for fish as opposed to heaving a weight. I don't know who approached who on this, but it was I who ended up with the job of pulling it off—the mission to develop a feature story of what it is like when a fisherman and distance caster conspire in the finest surf-casting water on the planet.

Docwra held six U.K. distance casting records in both conventional and fixed spool, one of which was 645 feet, having beat some of today's World Record holders. Standing at just under six feet, he was a slim man of roughly 35, who spoke in a strong, Cockney accent that was devoid of the H sound as well as drawing from a vocabulary that evoked endless questions from us and the kids. For instance, he repeatedly referred to the buggy as a "lowry," which caused the kids to view him as somewhat of a curiosity in spite of their immediate acceptance of this strange Englishman. We must have seemed an odd clutch to him, what with girls casting a tin squid over 300 feet and Sandra exaggerating the size of stripers with stories of fish capable of hauling a man into the sea. Now 14, the twins enjoyed leading poor Docwra to the areas where they knew that he would step on skates that were lying on the bottom. These would "fly" off when they felt his weight, upsetting his footing, the girls giggling as he danced in horror to escape the "magic carpets."

As his gamekeeper, it was imperative that I position him to take a good fish. Placing him at the head of the Chatham Inlet rip, his plug would be the first seen if and when the bass came through. Fishing just below him, I frequently checked his drag, fishing half-heartedly myself, watching for him to take his first fish. But it was not to be that first night, we taking only three fish in the twenties, all by the girls. Still, Docwra was impressed when he saw one of Susan's, a 25 pounder, that was bigger than any surf fish he had ever seen. His second night was one that he is not likely to forget.

The girls held as great a charm over the fish as they did over him and he insisted that he be placed beside them. Soon after sunset I heard him bellow for me above the sound of the surf and ran down to him with the gaff.

"Ey Frank," his conventional reel yielding the soft snapping sound of mono leaving the spool, "what 'ave I got 'ere, bloomin' alley-gator?"

He kept a tight line with the rod high, making the fish out, making no effort to store line as what seemed like a huge striper moved off with a power many of us have known. I've seen cows leave that Chatham rip many times before—and that is what he had, but it got off the plug disappointing us all.

Sandra landed a bluefish soon after that and she demonstrably placed a billy club in its maw chilling Docwra as the splinters crackled from its teeth. I was fishing a live eel about ten yards away when the shake and pause strike of a bluefish came to it. The thing went berserk when I set on it, splashing about in the surf, then beelining in on poor Docwra's knees, the sound and sight of the bluefish driving him out of the water in a frenzy. Having only frightened the bluefish in my effort to catch him, I pointed out to Dave that the fish had only been holding on to the eel, (showing him the half that remained) hoping that plausible explanation would soothe him. But between the loss of a great bass and the aggressive attack of the bluefish—when he had been trying to catch one all night—I know that inside he was capable to tilting a stress machine. Bad night.

Between his trans-Atlantic flight and two nights fishing until four, he was getting pretty groggy; most men would have fallen face down in the sand from exhaustion. Still, he slept fitfully, alternating between cigarettes and dreams of great fish. A short time after dawn, as he smoked outside the buggy, he gasped at the sight of a huge fish that lay trapped and struggling in the low tide shallows. When I rose, sometime later, he greeted me with a 23 pound cod.

" 'Ey Frank," he asked, "why would anyone in this country even to bother to learn to cast, when you can take fish like this—with your 'ands!"

Docwra's first bluefish came the third night amid a short blitz of mixed passing gamefish that were hurrying to Pleasant Bay. We were into it thick with Susan's drag groaning again from a good bass. Joyce had just switched rods, leaving a bluefish dry, and I had just fanned on a punch to my swimmer—wanting desperately to squeeze in another throw—when I saw the Englishman hauling back in the moonlight. His head would turn from the sea to us, to be certain that we knew, then his tip would strain as mono slipped away. By the time he had the blue in the wash, all of us had stopped fishing, and we coralled and kicked it high and dry.

Deep into the night we picked up a few more blues, the fish passing in small pods; Dick landed a decent striper around 18 pounds. Then, we toasted the sunrise, slept short, and drove north to P-Town.

Woolner had arranged for Charley Whitney, an old guard cohort of his, to take Dave out in the boat. Thus, the time we had left with the caster was limited.

Now, however, the pressure was off him because he had put some fish on the beach. Moreover, it became a recurrent joke that his best one had been taken with his bare hands. Of course, he knew that showing off his casting was necessary and that we all looked forward to seeing it. With things the way they were regulation wise, we had to stay at one of the "Self-Contained Areas" and the one we used was the largest—Race City. Here the campers are always stacked two, sometimes three deep from the water. Everybody knows everybody else's business and if they don't, they make it a point to find out. I introduced Dave to a few of the gang and it didn't take long for all of Race City to know that we had the U.K. casting champion with us.

His casting rods had been shipped to Charley Whitney and having them in his hands for the first time here seemed to transpose him into a different person. He fidgeted over them like a father, feeling their finish for signs of damage during the trip. These were huge sticks, 14 feet, with a lower section that was of aircraft aluminum that ferruled to fiberglass. But most of all it was the inscrutable transformation, the magic, that the sticks seemed to have over both of us. If I was intimidated, he certainly drew a measure of self-confidence from them. Long before he ever cast one of them, they had set about the task of making us equals.

In a way Docwra's very presence was viewed subjectively as an assault upon the self-esteem of every surfcaster in the Provincelands. But it shouldn't have been every surfcaster—only most. And, just as word had spread that we had the caster, I let it out that he was going to cast that afternoon. Some of the smarter ones wouldn't give me the satisfaction of showing him off. Still, I am certain that word of his impending exhibition had reached everybody.

We were certain of that when a surfman from Pennsylvania knocked on the buggy door asking right out when the Englishman was going to cast. I had assured Dave that there would be a crowd. And I could tell that it didn't matter to him, but he knew it mattered to me. Fighting a grin as I handed him the guides for taping, Joyce about choked on her beer when Docwra asked for a bit of lime. "Soon," I said, in a tone that implied that we had been disturbed. Then, as he left, I allowed him to hear that you can't do anything around here without all of Race City knowing it. Joyce served up a big dinner for the six of us—plenty of beer and pop—then we went outside to a gallery that had thickened to nearly all the people of the beach.

The moment that Docwra stepped out of the buggy and lifted the big stick from the bumper spike, all life at Race City seemed altered, transfixed, intimidated by what it was certain it was about to see. The Pennsylvanian motioned seaward with his arms at a tin boat that was returning from the east, its skipper trying to decipher what in hell this guy on the beach was gesturing about to him nearly a quarter mile out.

The caster was easily 30 feet from the water, his back to it, looking over the dunes for signs of wind. In a spoken tone, he announced to me, "A lob." I nodded to the Pennsylvanian who turned to the gallery.

"He's wetting the spool."

There was a rumble of voices and movement of heads.

Then, all went silent. Dave pivoted softly and drove the sinker maybe 450 feet, parting the sea surface so gently that most didn't know where it landed. The Pennsylvanian must have heard some disappointment among the crowd because he then admonished, in what was apparently an impatience that the Englishman was merely checking out his gear. Dave hung his head over the reel, rewinding carefully, laying each turn of mono on with total precision.

Then he carefully paced another five yards from the water, allowing the weight to hang down to the reel, measuring the distance from it to the tip.

"Least he could do is get near the friggin' water," someone said.

"Gentlemen, please," urged the Pennsylvanian, pressing his palms down in the thin air.

Docwra's eyes met mine, a subtle nod sought clearance that was barely perceptible as he waited for a response while he nervously hefted the casting rod. I looked at the Pennsylvanian with only a slight change in my focus, then dropped my chin ever so slightly.

He tossed the sinker in front of him toward the dunes, began a whirling arc while running toward the water, turning his body to follow the accelerating sinker as he circled in a run, each leg catching his forward and turning motion as he went. The caster covered the 40 feet in only a few seconds, the 14 foot East Anglian rocket launcher arced around his body, two fingers released the spool to its attack speed of 36,000 R.P.M., and the weight disappeared with a brisk report that sounded like a badly loaded small caliber rifle.

As his fingers tickled the spool to prevent the override, all heads turned to one another, each asking the other if they had seen it, and the man in the boat—out around 800 feet—just happened to glance seaward as though he

Imagine flying thousands of miles to a strange land because you are a good caster and then catch a 23 pound cod "with your 'ands."

were the only one who knew where it landed presenting the illusion that it had passed him. I lost all sight of it because Dave's exaggerated motion is such a distraction and the launch speed was so fast that even the rod is nothing but a blur. Still, I could never admit that, so I grinned in obvious satisfaction in the hope that our audience would blame themselves for failing to see such a notable event.

"He broke off," growled one observer.

But the Pennsylvanian, who was faking it as much as I, set him straight by pointing out that he was reeling in with tension.

"Where'd it go then?" one fisherman asked.

With that our emissary asked if Docwra would cast again, while I dropped a stage whisper to Dave about "a good 700 feet." I know that Dave was acknowledging the request for another cast, but this was understood to mean that he agreed that the throw had gone that far.

"Over 700 feet," the Pennsylvanian called to the crowd.

Rubbing his arms and shoulders like a handler, I whispered to Docwra, "How do ya' see the freakin' thing?" He cautioned me to watch it leave the beach, rather than watch for the splash, because there was just too much sea out there, too much distance, for an eye to pick up the splash.

The Pennsylvanian, myself, and the Englishman went through the same chain of command just before the latter let another go. Less than half of us saw this one splash down, but I saw it—roughly 600 feet. And Docwra, fully knowing of the game I played and that no doubt more of them had seen this one, put the rod down in disgust as a bad cast when in fact it was the kind of throw that had enshrined him in his homeland.

Small wonder that he could cast a weight over 1/10 of a mile. The forces have to be there, if you figure it out. The 14 foot rod with a 13 foot trail of line swings through a circle that measures 54 feet in diameter, without counting his arms. Like a sling, which can heave a small stone hard enough to kill a man, the centrifugal force is enormous! He claims that the sinker whirls at over 200 M.P.H. just before he lets go. Indeed, the force is so great that no man can thumb the spool in the way that conventional casters usually do. Were he to try, the caster would be cursed with slippage and false starts as the spool moved under his thumb during the all-important initial rotation. Docwra found that he had to lock the spool in position with two fingers, removing one of the reel's cross-bars to make room for them.

Writing for *Sea Angler*, a British sport fishing publication, 'Cassious' Fielden said, "The distances East Anglian anglers talk about when they are catching cod are like telephone numbers to us. I don't think I could see as far as some of these anglers cast."

Nor can I.

North Sea or English Channel, if you and I had to fish waters that were that devoid of fish, we would probably be wearing sneakers on a playing field and casting for distance ourselves. They have reason to celebrate when a conger eel or "sea basse," which is a different species and much smaller, is caught. Truth is that most English sea fishermen, if they are serious about the task, board a head boat to jig the wrecks. It seems that is where their technology is directed. When fishing this way, they lower a one pound drail, give or take ounces to accommodate currents, with a whole lot of teasers attached.

On his last day with us, our casting champion was packing his things, no doubt with the thought of how he could make his duffel lighter. He handed me a few spiked sinkers, an artifact which I had never seen. And then he held out a curiosity which he claimed had stormed British wreck fishing.

Telling me the story which I just told you about using teasers, he said that they had been through the small surgical tube lures but that these were a cut above. Our eel fly droppers were on his mind because we had made much of them and he too had taken fish on them.

"Frank," he said, making certain that he had my attention, "with all the teaser fishing that you 'ave, might these do?"

With that he handed me some five inch molded rubber sand eels that were as close a likeness as I had ever seen. They were equipped with a stainless hook and had a small swimmer plate in the tail, which I later found caused the lure to vibrate from the force of passing water. Practically weightless, these "Red Gills," as they are called, were certain to be an effective teaser.

That day, just before we packed him to town for the Boston ferry, we talked of his trip, promising to write, to meet again. Though he was haggard from the mid watch hunts with me by night and boat fishing with Charley Whitney by day, he was alert enough to spot a whale surfacing a half mile offshore at a submarine gradient that we call the pot line, her spout rising and bending in the sou'west like windblown steam.

"That's a might of fish," he said, "You see, Frank, you can always do with a bit more of a cast."

CHAPTER 13

Even Fathers Cry

Dickie was gone now. We gave him to the Coast Guard recruiter in Providence that spring, with tear filled eyes that so desperately tried to say, as so many parents before, "Take care of our son."

Still, there was a part of me that did not seem to know that he was at Cape May. Nights at Chatham Inlet, I would look around the buggy for him at sunset wanting him to take his position up tide. There were even times when I thought that I heard his whistle above the sweep and hiss of the waves that hurried past. But these were mere tears of the heart, the leftover trappings of a father's mind that refused to face the reality of time. We had been such a team.

What tricks of Nature does He play upon us. When the world was young, when Dick weighed nothing more than a schoolie, I had felt his naked body against my chest and remembered dearly how he seemed to delight in the feel of flesh against his. Memories of when I would stick a finger in his mouth to get a rise out of Joyce, while she heated a bottle, danced in my mind; the boyhood surfrods; Pochet; all the kills and payoffs. It seemed that there were things of his everywhere in the buggy that had been left there to either make good his memory or torment my sense of filial order. His boyish kit—a small sheath bound knife, a hand gaff and pliers—so evoked the memories of 10 years of surf fishing that I stowed them deep in the valise of the camper out of sight one night ... then cried. Why is it that they remain our babies while someone else can coldly measure their bodies of six feet and declare them fit men for the service of their nation? Is it they who do not recognize mere boys, or fathers who fail, or refuse, to acknowledge manhood?

In the time that Dick had been with us the average weight of our bass had more than doubled. We still had the 16-fish-to-the-box schoolies, which were small enough to make the big money cull of 90 cents. And commonly about half our catch was a spread on up to commonly the high twenty pound range which paid as low as 60 cents. I had thought that our total poundage would drop off with the boy gone, but so many things were changing to improve our catches that the numbers rose instead.

We added a used chase vehicle, a '72 Scout, which was a scary $2400 investment against fish checks. Yet, we paid for it the first half of the '76 season. That little four wheeler had been around, but it had never stunk of the fish that it did once it had been with us a few weeks. What with all the regulation dodging that we had learned to do, the small buggy broadened our options to the limit.

For instance, we would take it to Nauset Beach on a Monday night to check the inlet out. If it was any good, we came back Tuesday night with the big camper for 72 hours. By doing that our absence in P-Town created the illusion that we were playing it straight with the Seashore Park regulation of limiting families to 21 days per summer. If, after three nights, Nauset was still profitable, I would write us a bogus pass for P-Town, camp in there by day for sleep, then go back to Nauset each night with the case. With two buggies, we could fish either Nauset or P-Town as long as the fish held up. Lots of times, it would be the other way and we wouldn't get back to Nauset for maybe 10 nights. But usually between the Race and Chatham Inlet we

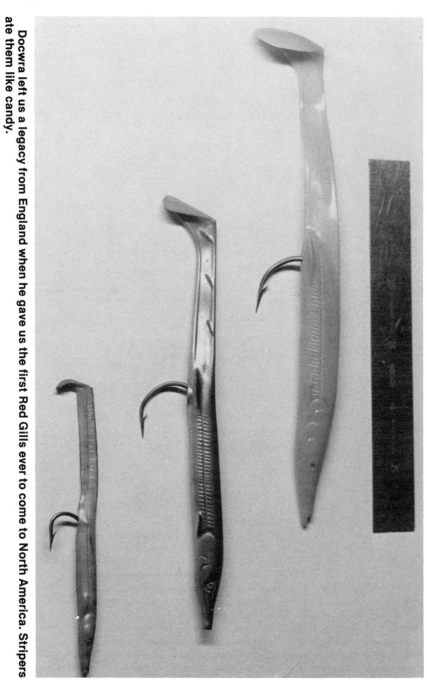

Docwra left us a legacy from England when he gave us the first Red Gills ever to come to North America. Stripers ate them like candy.

had some serious poundage on the go. We had become so mobile that nobody who knew somebody who knew enough about what we were doing to want to look could find us. We had become Cape Cod shadows of the night, losing our profile in this grand shuffle of time and beaches. We never cheated enough to bring attention to ourselves; we never talked enough for others to know how the fishing was; we left small enough drops of fish on slips in full view of the snoopers to make them comfortable in the thought that fishing for Frank Daignault was a dismal, low average.

Moreover, the economic oppression of feeding and caring for a basket-ball team was abating. Joyce had finished college and was teaching, there were no car payments, and the fish money was all gravy. We had an account at Cape Cod Bank and Trust where we dumped the checks weekly. I had been writing so many articles about surfcasting winters, that I was beginning to enjoy a measure of importance in the sport fishing fraternity. Tackle manufacturers were sending me stuff faster than the five of us could lose it. Free monofilament. Free Rebels. Discounted waders. I sent a couple of pages of slides to Woolner who took two and mailed me a check for $400!

Life is a lot like the banks that will lend anybody who doesn't need it all the money they want. When we didn't have a window to throw it out of, we had to put a dime in a machine just for a pee. Now, that it was becoming apparent that we weren't hurting, we weren't paying for anything any more. Then there is the business of making money.

When you come from an industrial society, where you are paid according to what you can give your employer, a kind of decay of ethic is inevitable. You soon learn to think that the ultimate accomplishment is to be paid for doing nothing. Everybody, it seems, is looking to make the big hit of disability or unemployment so that they can sit around and get paid for it. But they are only products of the frustration of knowing that if you are not ever going to get rich, you may as well be happy. And to them being happy is having a few bucks and not having to work. But I submit that the ultimate of that demented, convoluted thought pattern is not a steady check which is small—payment for even smaller services—it is to be paid to play. We played until the salt burned the cuts made from handling striped bass. We played until our legs ached. We played from when the sun dipped in the western sky until it magically reappeared again in the east, making us wonder how it could have speeded up so while it was on the other side. We gutted, rinsed, sweated, schemed, sniffed, listened, watched with only one thought: Where and how can we catch more striped bass?

Maybe that is why those rubber things, the Red Gills, as Docwra had called them, had taken such a hold upon my mind. Any place where we found bass there were always sand eels, either schooled and massed enough so as to make the sea appear stained from their numbers or dug in so that they would scoot from the feel of a boot grinding the sand pebbles together. Here, this English caster hands me a perfect rendition, nine in all, of this very baitfish. It is the moldmakers art of a perfect sand eel with a long snout for digging, little folded pectorals, the slimness, even the proportion and more important, the size, of what is disgorged when a lineside is hauled up on the beach. So perfect in its imitation, except for the swimmer plate in the tail that gives it its life, it makes you want to joke about the possibility that a real bait will try to mount it as it passes in its appointed mission of fooling something far more important.

One night, when the sou'west humped white past Race Point Station, fish could be seen in the wash with every revolution of the light. Joyce and I rousted the girls from their bunks in the big buggy. Susan came out first

Every father likes having a son to bring along in the surfcasting game.
Guess I was just plain lucky.

Sons grow up fast and it becomes time for them to go their own way.

Once I started writing about fishing I could spend winters telling of what we had learned.

with her pajamas rolled above her knees. Next time I looked, both she—one leg of her pajamas down in the wash—and Sandra were into fish. And I walked among them like an athletic coach urging them on and reminding them to report the first bluefish. With only nine Red Gills in the western hemisphere, it would be I who would snip them from the leaders! Carol, last, and running the wrong way for the bumper spikes, leaped out of the way when I moved the chase west toward where the girls had gathered. Joyce was dragging a brute from the slowly covering bar; Susan gave me one flash from her light unnecessarily; and, Sandra was back in action because her fish had come off the teaser easily. Carol ran, this time in the right direction. I walked among the big bass now strewn along the bar, wielding a billy and heaving them into the Scout.

Susan, who had been doing so well, had her fishing go sour and I discovered that her Red Gill was gone. Later, it was the plug of one of the others. It took some time for it to sink in with me as to why things were missing for no apparent reason. What was happening was that the kids would hook a fish and while it was running, another would take the remaining lure. Once there were two bass, they seemed to blame one another for their predicament, fighting each other so that the surf virtually exploded until the leader broke between them. Poor Carol, nearly in tears, hadn't hooked a fish. It was time to end the control of the experiment and give the darling thing a Red Gill like her sisters.

In just the few minutes that I needed to change Carol's tackle over, add a Red Gill, production demands were backing up with rods dancing in the front bumper. The girls were wearing down from the action, the twins bitching at one another over whose spot it was that they both took fish from. Clearly, in the rhythmic burst of Race Light, you could see an ever so slight impression where the sea broke over the sou'west corner. It was a hole about 40 feet long, maybe a foot deeper than the rest of the shoreline, but enough structure to appeal to baitfish and the frantic stripers in the area knew it. Susan had been using it all along, but had not met Sandra because the accident of timing had prevented them from being there at the same time. When one was casting, the other would be following a hooked fish east, they alternatingly taking from the same yard of surf. Now, as time would have it, they were working it together ... and that is how they hooked up.

A rising sea washed over Carol's sneakers as I slammed a 40 pounder into the cooler. Sandra slid a fish of half that to the tailgate, preventing me from moving the little chase to drier ground. Her Red Gill was cut from the cartilage of the fish's maw, loaded, and, just as I was revving the machine, Joyce spiked an empty rod, the mono straightening in the wind from a break off. Carol was on.

Accelerating through a puddle of backwater, I gunned the machine part way up the beach incline then killed it quickly trying to save every yard that these fish would be dragged. Joyce had a spare rod in her hands when I came down to walk among them.

"Keep casting, hold back your speed, easy Sandra," as she set on a take. "Keep casting. We got their number."

Poor Susan looked to be at near exhaustion when she beached her fish. No small wonder, as she probably had fought and dragged over two boxes herself. Still, Carol had followed hers so far east toward the Traps that I had to leave them all to pick her up with the chase. When I got there she was ducking the steel of the plug as her bass strained to rid itself of the teaser hook that was imbedded in its tail.

When we got back to the others, there were no fish on the beach and nobody was fighting one. The tide had again driven us back from where we could have taken more. I always feel cheated when that happens because as long as there is a pound of energy in any of us, I would prefer to cast on. One never knows when it will be like this again. When I think of how the others, who dream their dreams of great fish dashing through the side of a foaming wave just before it falls spent against the shore, I remember how lucky we are to have it this way together.

CHAPTER 14

Beach Erosion and Terns

In the few years that we had been in P-Town the number of oversand vehicle permits issued had tripled. Park management had tightened the enforcement of every regulation that formerly had been enforced loosely. Self-Contained Areas, where the campers had been parked, were abolished at the rate of one per year. Herring Cove was the first, then Race Point, and the most easterly, Highhead.

These changes, however, had no effect upon our operation because we could go anywhere with a chase. It was not important where we slept, only where we fished. But all oversand use had been under fire to some degree. There had been a study conducted by U-Mass. that concluded that the beach environment had no capacity for oversand vehicle use. Meanwhile, a lot of townies were lobbying for the abolition of the buggies citing this scientific study. Equipped with photos of buggy tracks that climbed up dunes, obviously destroying grass, there were frequent editorials in Cape papers that urged closure or, at the least, greater control.

Of course the whole thing was a sham because the study done by this Massachusetts college was funded by the Federal Government. Years before, Richard Nixon had issued an edict against all off-road vehicles; this was based upon abuses in inland national parks, like Yosemite or Yellowstone, and the Park Service was simply tightening the screws. Any manager who knows that he is going to encounter resistance, is smart enough to back his moves with a scientific study. Naturally, I could never know if the University of Massachusetts was told what conclusion to bring in when they were finished. But it is a dead cinch that if somebody is told to do something, they can also be told what results to get. One thing that makes me suspect that that is exactly what was done was the amateurish science that was practiced when these biologists sought to determine if driving on the flats at Hatches Harbor would be detrimental to the shellfish there. Try to envision Doctor Greenleaf and his assistant, Ms. Pettiwhack, burying clams in the sand, then driving a Wagoneer over them to see if doing so hurts them.

Whatever happened to the clams, the Park Service decided that driving below the high water mark was detrimental to the shellfish. Do you think that the fact that there are no shellfish indigenous to the 40 miles of shoreline in the Park was a consideration? Nobody wanted to drive in Hatches Harbor, a tiny estuary where clams do live. Thus, the study was conducted in the wrong place, yet acted as a basis for another. I'm not saying that these "scientists" didn't know what they were doing; they knew all along what they were doing: They were capitulating to what the park wanted in their plan for greater control.

Two considerations were utilized by so-called environmentalists to attack oversand vehicle use: Destruction of the dune grass, which is what holds the *terra* firm preventing wind and sea erosion; and, disturbing of nesting sights for the shore bird that all surfcasters have learned to love, the least tern. Admittedly, nobody ever said that mobile surfcasters were the cause of the tern's endangerment, but the feeling that the species needed all the help it could get was without dispute. Let's talk about the first.

The Cape Cod National Seashore's Provincelands area is a maze of dune

When I think of how others dream of fish dashing in the surf I knew our family was lucky to share what we did together.

trails which lead to this point or that along the beach. When a surfcaster has an area in mind, do you think that he is interested in using one of these dune roads? He would be a fool to option one because to do so is to deprive himself of the opportunity to view the surf as he goes. Viewing the surf is how one often comes upon feeding stripers or bluefish. On the other hand, the boys with the rollbars and girlfriends who want to show off their driving prowess require the challenge of a hill and dale trail. Here, in the solitude of the Provincelands, they can check their mirrors, look ahead, then cut the wheels and give their little CJ a real work-out, tearing up the priceless dune-grass in the process.

Moreover, the advent of the "dune-buggy," which is a western aberration that was never intended to be used in fragile coastal, erosion sensitive environments, had come to the New England shore. An intense marketing program touted the hot looking Volkswagons with fiberglass bodies and over-size tires as the way to go, complete with a buxom, scantilly clad female passenger. I visited one of these "speedshops" in Rhode Island and was told that there were miles of dunes on Cape Cod where a driver could put one through its paces. When I questioned the legality of this, the owner/manager told me that problem was only in Rhode Island.

To the uninitiated, there is little or no difference between a beach buggy and a dune buggy. It is one of those traps of language that forsakes meaning which somehow defies solution. All my life I had friends say, "Are you going fishing in your dune buggy?" The beach buggy came about as a means for surfcasters to more effectively move about the shore while fishing; the dune buggy was an inland toy like a trail bike or ATV. The lumping comes about out of ignorance.

Riding in the dunes cannot be done without the clear evidence of tracks and the environmental damage that comes with them. With such behavior so undesirable, why then didn't the Park Service close all so-called dune trails and stop leading the public at large to sin? Instead, they sought to curtail all oversand vehicle use, punishing the largest user group for the behavior of a few who had been led by their own mismanagement.

If the Park Service had been sincere in its efforts, it would have routed traffic to the sea edge, where no environmental damage, no erosion, takes place as a consequence of vehicular traffic. Now the birds.

Mid-July on, particularly at night, we have always watched the trails for the little terns that have just left the nest. The little fluff balls characteristically get caught in the rut of the trail and struggle to mount the track edges to flee a vehicle, falling and winging it badly to escape. All of us, as well as the generation before, would stop our buggies to shoo their little butts out of the way. We like the birds, not simply because they are a part of what Nature has granted us, but because, as adults, they will wheel and dive over baitfish and contribute greatly in our search for gamefish.

But these have been hard times for the terns and wildlife authorities have been concerned with the survival of the species. Once there were vast colonies of nesting terns all along the beach; now there are only small, sparsely populated groups of them in a place where the most favorable breeding conditions anywhere on the continent can be found. Consequently, Park officials mark off nesting sites by driving stakes and running line along them. So much effort has been put into protecting nesting terns that the Park Service has a biologist assigned to the program just for CCNS.

Naturally, when someone in charge of such things finds a nestling that has strayed into the track crushed, there is hell to pay. That is why just under two miles of beach from Highhead west was closed to all traffic for the duration of the nesting season. When this came about, around ten of us went before the North District Ranger to ask questions.

His explanation was that with the least tern on the verge of endangered status, there could be no tolerance for vehicle-caused kills. It was a hard case to fight in view of the fact that there indeed might have been some fluffball mortality. However, it ended in compromise where officials agreed to escort surfcasters nightly if they wanted to fish the area. It was after the formal discussion and agreement on the matter that the biologist concurred with one of the surfmen who said he had seen a fox on that stretch of beach, earlier, before hatching of the chicks.

"The fox," the biologist admitted, "has been hammering the chicks. First, it was the eggs and now it kills what few have hatched out."

"Wait a minute," one of the New Yorkers interjected, "are you telling us that we are being kept out of there because somebody ran over ONE chick with their buggy, and a goddamn fox is having omelets every morning?"

Once the realization of this hit home with the surfmen, the meeting went from cordial negotiation to near riot. Some of the boys, who were about ready to leave, came back into the meeting and the realization that we were being taken was hitting us all at once.

"Shoot the #?!@†:+?! fox!"

"We can't," the biologist insisted, straining to muster his most persuasive tone. "That would require an Environmental Impact Statement and the nesting season will be over by the time we get one."

"All you need is a hunting license."

"Gentlemen," the North District Ranger interjected, "It is illegal to hunt in the Provincelands and I am charged with the management of its wildlife resources. I intend to see that is done to the letter of the law."

Of course nobody who was there knew that the fox season was closed, not even those charged with the care of wildlife resources. But if such a fox were raiding the chickens of a local farmer, it could have been dispatched legally after one phone call.

However, there is a failing to all the reasoning that we speak of here. Such reasoning supposes that the Park Service is serious about the protection of the least tern. What they were serious about, was creating the illusion that they were caring for the terns and that oversand vehicle use was a threat to the birds.

The fox was but one player in a cast of thousands of predators that have ravaged the nests of all shore birds beyond a sustaining level. The presence of man has enhanced the foraging opportunities of seagulls to the point where they can be found feeding behind every inland restaurant and schoolyard hundreds of miles from the shore. Indeed, the coastline is so overpopulated with them that there are no longer enough tern eggs to sustain them. But when the U.S. Fish and Wildlife Service planned to poison 5,000 to 10,000 gulls on Monomoy Island, a rookery which covers with gulls nightly at the expense of other species, it was the same preservationists that were kicking the buggies off the beach who succeeded in preventing the measure.

Our society is now ruled by a generation of Disney-trained amateur wildlife managers who so outnumber the trained professionals, who wield such political clout, that public support for putting down the gulls, killing them, is unattainable.

Beach resources are more a case of user groups jealously seeking all they can get for themselves. The average Cape Codder, who himself has come from somewhere else, wants to be able to walk the beaches free from the stench of exhaust fumes, and the insecurity of passing motor vehicles. Even though there are few people who use the vast, uninhabited miles of shore on the Cape on foot, theirs is a point with a measure of validity. As for environmental damage by vehicles that use the flat zone between the berm and dune edge, above the high water mark, neither side really believes that such damage takes place. If they did, there would not be so many motorized ranger patrols daily, each day of the calendar year.

When it looked like the hurricane was bearing down on us, Race City was evacuated to the parking lot off the beach.

CHAPTER 15

Hurricane

When the Petty Officer of the watch hoisted the second storm flag at the Coast Guard station in town, none of us were surprised. There had been some talk the night before that a hurricane was coming up the coast. Now its status had been upgraded from Watch to Warning. Of course when word of this was received by the North District Ranger, he ordered all the self-contained vehicles off the beach.

Within an hour the hundred odd families were out of Race City towing their boats, the husbands driving the big rigs and the wives behind the wheels of the chases. The caravan of walk-ins and pickup campers ended at the Race Beach parking lot spilling kids all over the place who excitedly asked questions about the impending storm. Still, there wasn't a cloud in the sky, but there was a humid, almost stagnant pungency to the air. I went back to bed.

Two hours later, Carol told me that she had talked to Vince and had seen Conrad going out on the beach. Unable to bear the thought that somebody might be doing it without me, I slid into hippers and whipped the Scout west. By then a south wind had freshened over the dunes and I could make out that the tide force down from Race Light was stronger than usual. Once on the waterline trail, I could see several small four wheelers gathered at the Second Rip beside a line of casters, two leaning into fish and another bent over the sand beside this buggy. Out from the bank, a few bursts of white. Bluefish.

What a time this would be to take in a good load of bluefish. So often it is not what you catch, but what you are paid. Late summer, blues can go as low as eight cents per pound. Then, unaccountably, through some mystery of supply and demand, they can be 15. But rarely, these days, were they worth fishing for because they can tear up more equipment than the price that they bring at the dock. It only takes the ruination of one load of braided micron, or the loss of two plugs, to burn up the take from the first box of fish. We avoided them, selling only what was incidental to our striper fishing. But today was a different story, what with the entire East Coast commercial fishery battened down for the hurricane. In two days, the storm gone, there would be a lot of fish markets looking for something to put on the shelves. We had seen this before and knew that bluefish might make 30 cents—well worth the effort when they are all over the place.

The Striper Swiper sailed easily with the wind behind and I snubbed the spool to tighten the line just before it landed, threw the clutch, then started the rhythmic popping. A swirl developed behind it, then another, just before the line lifted from the oily sea. On then off. The popper skittered from the sudden loss in tension, but before I could reel up the slack, another blue took it down. Meanwhile, Vince, Conrad and the others whom I did not know, were all hauling. Line snapped from the drag, my fish sounding and lunging seaward; then it was off. Running backwards, I fought the current to get the popper back to the surface where it threw water once before being inhaled. Vince was batting his fish and Conrad kicking his. More dry line left the spool as my bluefish ran. Vince was on again! Then my fish broke the surface once and was off. Conrad hauled back on another. Now, with my plug on the top, I had it popping quickly, yet never saw the take. On. Conrad was backing. Now when the line left my spool, serious concerns came to mind as to whether or not I might run out. These bluefish were playing a relay game with my plug and I wasn't doing too well. This last fish was so far out when it broke that I didn't believe it was mine.

Leaden clouds scudded over the dune tops, the wind seeming to pick up. Conrad was bent over in the sand, Vince was chasing in the surf, one guy was smoking a cigarette, and all the others were fighting fish. My first blue had been brought to within 200 feet of my furthest cast. Then Conrad dropped a short lob 20 feet, popped it twice, hooked up and backed the chopper onto the sand. I managed five turns. What in hell was I doing in the freaking shipping lanes with all these fish against the beach? They had fish laying all over the place and I, with a 45 pound line, still hadn't land a fish.

I horsed backwards toward the buggy, spiked the rod, picked up another, layed it short, and gasped at the sight of frantic lunges. At last we were open for business.

Now the wind was gusting at 50, the clouds appearing to labor their way into closing the gap between them as they cleared the dunes. I had three on the sand, the other stick still bouncing from the relay fish. A few raindrops made their way across my fore, then stopped. The others were cleaning up the beach, preparing to leave. I bounced another blue to the sand, then fought my way into an oilskin slicker that was stiff from the heat of the buggy.

Vince jazzed his Bronco, calling to me to leave the poor fish alone, and Conrad threw me a half wave, half salute. The others must have left while I was engaged. By now the monotony of jostling with bluefish had taken hold, allowing my mind to ponder the storm.

What is a hurricane like? How do they come? Is it a progressive thing, or does the tempest come over the top of the grass, upon you so suddenly that there is no time to reach shelter? If it does, when it does, is it enough to push a man into the water? Why were the others gone? In either direction there was neither man nor buggy. Race City had certainly proven its mobility. A Wrigleys wrapper scurried past from my right, the only evidence that man, other than myself, had been there in a hundred years. On the outside, I could see the lines of white caps heading west. The surf had started to bulge more now, a sweep shoving on my hippers sending water onto my trousers.

Only the snap was showing on this bluefish, so I opened it and left the plug so as to put on another. Dropping my cast short, at the end of the sweep, I allowed it to laze long enough for it to be eaten. It gets no easier than this.

Still, the impending storm had taken a positive hold upon my mind. I wanted to forget the eerie fear that the air was giving me. How can the wind blow so hard, in such an open place, yet taste so foul, so stagnant. Even the rain, now pelting at a steady rate from the southeast, did nothing to cleanse it. The horrors were taking over. With the buggy facing the east, this hard driving rain could find its way, somehow, into the wires. I could picture myself walking out, but what of the Scout laying on the beach in a hurricane? Would it be there when I came back? *Screw this,* I thought.

Tidying up the yard, I bounced the bluefish two at a time into the box. Now that I had decided, I couldn't get the hell out of there fast enough. Race Station had disappeared in a shroud of gray, there were no boats at sea, no planes in the sky. I could read the headlines: "Man Dies in Cape Hurricane."

I was running now, picking up the pliers, billy, and knife thinking out loud, for who could hear. "I am getting the f--- out of here."

The Scout was not wet, only my pants. The track was not windblown soft, it was windblown hard and easy going. I made beautiful time until I recognized that one of the surfrods was bending more than even a hurricane wind might do. I had neglected to reel in my shipping lane, relay fish. The thought crossed my mind to cut it, for I had no stomach for one last bluefish. But 30 cents a pound was a five dollar bill here. I cranked and pumped, then snubbed down the star on the squidder to put on some serious line. In no time I had the exhausted blue in the wash, maybe 15 pounds. I could see the yellow tint of his belly when I lifted the rod in time with a bulge in the surf. Then the plug came back over my shoulder.

Whipping the family chase, you would have thought that somebody was out for my life and I covered the mile of beach in scant seconds. And when I climbed the last dune hill of the trail, I slowed it down to a lazy ride for all to see how easy it is to push a hurricane.

The temporary Race City was buttoned tight, the buggies crowded together both for space and breaking the wind. Joyce and the girls didn't let anyone see them, but they were glad that I was back. I drank a little whisky, then climbed into a soft and warm bag in the top bunk for a sleep of dreams.

I don't know how long I was out, maybe two hours, when a roar, accompanied by a pause in the rain, woke me while the buggy listed on its springs. No doubt what we felt was the 90 mile gust that Chatham radar reported later. The recent advisories had placed the storm center at the mouth of the Connecticut River with winds on the outside well east of the Cape. There was relief that we were being spared the full force of the hurricane, what little we did have passing quickly. By early afternoon the rain had stopped and everybody was anxious to get back out on the beach, wondering if they were going to be credited with a half day for the time spent in the parking lot.

The passage of all this low pressure caused a surge of wind out of the sou'west that I knew would have Race Point in a dither. But everybody was standing around kicking tires, waiting for clearance from the authorities. We fired up the two machines amid a torrent of "It's guys like you that spoil it for everybody" and went fishing. Somebody had to make certain the beach was safe.

Cutting the first track through what had been Race City, and soon would be again, was a strange, lonely feeling similar to that which had driven me out of there last time out. I backed the big truck away from the waterline, leaving it for the boatmen, Joyce shut the Scout down, and we leveled the camper. Then, in my most authoritative voice, "I hereby proclaim this here beach, all its entitlements, all that the eye can see, as Daignault-land." Whereupon the girls applauded and Joyce rolled her eyes because that is what mothers are supposed to do when fathers act like children.

Joyce and I were suited into waders and oilskin tops within minutes. When we rounded the curve in the beach at Race Light, we could clearly see the water still heaving from the storm, the wind pushing the tops off the foamers down the front side so that everything was white. Thousands of the big clumsy gulls hovered, dove, then hurried only to change direction as if unable to sort what part of the blitz they wanted to be in. It was the most delicious mess a surfcaster ever saw! We were on right away, Joyce straining to get a fish up, then a wave broke and her ankle deep water went waist deep and her 12-ish school bass was behind her. We kept this up for an hour, the fish roughly half blues, when Paulie Hoercher pulled up beside us on low beach.

"Hello Nutbag," he said, "I knew it had to be you that cut the track."

"Find your own blitz," I told him, and with that he kissed Joyce, as he always does, and went to work with us.

My friend Paulie Hoercher who was the official cat-saver of the New York Fire Department. He is so small that 55 pounders look like world records.

Paulie, beautiful Paulie, a New Yorker that we had come to love. When he came in from the city, he always stopped to read my pulse. As a N.Y. fireman, he would trade vacation, fill in for other firefighters trading days, wangling, finagling, to spend more of his life in the Cape surf. He would be with us for weeks, disappear for a week, then be back on another vacation. I used to tell him that I hated the thought that all those New York City cats were not safe while he was on Cape Cod because, what with his tiny, 5 foot four inch frame, he was the official cat saver of the department. But that was only part of him because when on the Cape he was a pair of balls in waders that would disappear in the foam, then pop into view while talking himself in a trance, driving plugs over the wave tops.

The thing got so crazy and we got so haggard that we started to ease off from the frantic pace of the fishing. The wind had dropped off enough, in three hours, for us to remove the sinkers from ahead of the Red Gills and use plugs for casting weight. Well into our third box of fish, Joyce had a double going—one on the popper and another on the teaser. Her pair of stripers in the low thirties appeared to be fighting each other as Paulie and I heckled her while she strained to subdue them both in the surf. With the tide turning around 4:00 p.m., I started cleaning up because I didn't want to be caught loading fish while trying to move the buggy up from the water. It's important that the vehicle be as close as possible for tools, rod changes, and fish boxing because every second and every step counts in a blitz like this. Then the tide is dropping, you can leave a trail of fish and tools following the water down; but, with a coming tide, you have to watch the relationship of the water more closely. Moreover, the rise in water is not linear with time. Once the tide is two hours in, the rise in water is more dramatic so that it covers and sweeps things away. You can hook a good fish, line leaving against the drag, and before you know it the water is breaking against your wheels. After that, one bad splash and your ignition is doused. Of course, you don't have to take such chances, but your production will go down.

We hadn't eaten for seven hours, my waders were full of water, and my hands were getting like hamburger and burning from all the little cuts aggravated by the salt. Joyce drove the Scout back to the big buggy and got us some Twinkies and cold beer while the girls unloaded the boxes. Coming back she swung in a little too close to the surf and a wave washed the passenger door, hissing on the exhaust system; because of that she scooted farther up the bank than I would have liked. Nearly eating the cellophane on the first goodie, I offered Paulie a Twinkie if he promised to move downwind 1000 feet. And he, putting his arm around my Joyce warmly, offered her a better life with a "real fisherman."

The wind was pansying out by now and the Race had a good 50 casters spread, tonging. Roughly another box of fish and things had slowed because the rising water had moved us too far back. Fearing that some of our catch might spoil, we decided to load everything and head for the dock. Back at the buggy, the girls were gutting bluefish in their bathing suits.

"Yuck," Sandra blurted, as she pulled on a handful of bluefish entrails. Then Susan heaved a bloody organ at her twin and the guts war was on. Each of them had a bluefish by the tail and was reaching inside for more offal to throw at the other.

"This is the liver, this is the heart, here is the part that makes him ..."

And she threw a mushy, reddish organ that splatted in the knee deep wash beside Carol, who was the only one of them doing anything.

Pulling up beside them, I warned that they had better have the fish ready because the dock would be locked up within the hour. Then I slid another box onto the sand and ran the knife from vent to gill covers on what remained.

Our drop for the afternoon, including the box plus of blues taken before the storm, was just under 600 pounds; cull on the bass was 290 of jumbo. We didn't know the prices but the total value had to be close to $500.

Joyce had prepared pasta for dinner but pointed out that no buggies had come down from the Race, not even those she had seen drive past while I was at the dock. Shutting the stove down, she hopped into the Scout with me and we hurried west. Now the tide was really humping past the Race, with most of the rigs moved to the high water mark. Others were picking up gear and fish, their exhaust drifting from their buggies, for a last move. Nobody was standing around and quite a few of them were fighting fish—all bass. Paulie was panting on the hood of his Jeep, lamenting the high percentage of bluefish:

"Should have stayed, Nutbag, we been mohawking them."

Within three casts I had a bass on and turned to see Joyce carrying her rod with mono trailing back to the bumper spikes for another. Then she hooked up.

Compared to the pace of early afternoon, things were a little slower but still productive. The wind seemed to stay on a steady 20 knots sou'west, which were perfect conditions. But Joyce was pale from the continuous action and I could tell that she was worried about the girls. She went back in the chase and I stayed with Paulie for another hour but it was over.

Race City was back to its old self, fish-boxes, boat trailers. Those who were staying had taken their boats off. Nobody was around, however, probably eating or sleeping. Broken clouds still hurried over the dunes, the sun lowering. My stomach was gnawing on my back bone, especially once I smelled the gravy heating.

"The girls ate all the Fritos," Joyce lamented.

"They did," I said, trying to sound like a concerned father. "How about the Ring Dings?"

Rolling her eyes, she motioned to the hamburger and I swept my arm telling her to cook it all.

"Ever see such fish?" I said.

"I wish they would move out. This is too much!"

God, I love spaghetti and hamburger. I was dragging Portuguese bread through the rich, red gravy, saving the last patty for one final assault when Carol bounded in:

"MrHoercherisonandIgotathirtyfivepounderatmaxistruck ... and" ... pant, pant.

"Carol, for crying out loud, slow down!"

"Mister Hoercher is on and I got a 35 pounder at Mr. ..."

Joyce was adamant: "I'm through fishing."

Sliding into hippers, it was full dark when I came out. Paulie was tearing through everything in his buggy, a sure sign that things were moving. I felt a turn on my plug, clear sign that something had passed near it. I paused, rolled a few cranks on the squidder, then hauled back on the take. I heard Paulie's billy thump on a fish and the twins were running toward me from down the beach, but they slowed down once they realized that I was in the water. Not that it was heavy, every-cast-blitz, but we had stripers in the 30s for about two hours until after high water. Once the Second Rip died out, the linesides were gone and the bluefish moved in.

This caused most of the others to rack their surfrods. They were tired, as well as conscious of how unprofitable the choppers can be. But I couldn't shake the notion that these blues might be the best priced ones that we had ever seen. If it turned out that P-Town fish were all that came in at Fulton

Street, bids would skyrocket. I bent wire leaders to every rod on the Scout for some easy money. Dropping the tailgate, I opened a case of Gibbs Swimmers and armed every stick.

Sandra came by first but she couldn't reach them. I cast her rod, passed it to her and she hooked up. Susan saw this and went after Carol before she joined us. Mom was 20 feet behind Carol. In spite of a favorable wind, none of them could reach the concentration and all casts made by them went dry. Now all four of them waited with rods for me to cast and them to hook up. It was the first time that we had ever done the fish that way, but when something is working and you have the space ...

After midnight our bluefish left and all the girls went to bed. Joyce was haggard, but I couldn't come down. It is a thing that I hate about blitz. You would think that with all the action we had that I would fall into my bag and lapse into unconsciousness. But just the opposite happens. Somehow, I need the reassurance that there is nothing happening somewhere without me. You won't get it from Paulie.

"Hey Nutbag," Paulie said, sliding gear to the inside so that he could close his tailgate, "the Race is down enough."

"I'm not going to be a pig about it." using as matter-of-fact a voice as I could muster, "we just want a few fish for the freezer. Enough is enough."

I was going to the Race and Paulie knew it.

Right after the Traps, there was enough light from the lighthouse to illuminate Paulie's buggy, the only buggy, on the flats. Each time it made a rotation, I could see how his rig was low on the springs from the weight of what he had. Then we both dropped below the crest of the beach and slid softly the 400 feet to the water without lights. Joyce's head rolled forward in a bow causing her to react for an instant before sagging into a heap against her door. Some women just don't have any balls.

Blankets of sand eels sprinkled in the gentle surf and a thing moved among them. Paulie saw it. Paulie was into them right away because I had to remove the wire and clip on swimmers and Red Gills. Joyce got up on the third bang on her door, but she moved in a way that seemed to be hoping that they would be gone by the time she got there. Still, she beached a 41 pounder and a few others in the mid-20s. Paulie was loaded, all bass. The Scout was bottomed out on its springs and we had more fish at the big truck. The bluefish poundage was slightly higher than what we had in bass, but they went off at 28 cents per pound. My mental cash register was saturated. I couldn't figure out what we had but we were pushing a ton in all and the check was close to a $1,000.

Another fine friend and eminent surfcaster, John Valentine. I first learned of that great year from him.

CHAPTER 16

Blitz

We jump started the camper the last week in May. Wind was east and the Race City surf was big and dirty. Still, there was a season that we had to shake the gear down for, a mouse that had munched on some soap to kick out of the buggy and old friends to greet. New this season was a '77 Blazer right out of the showroom; it was the very first new motor vehicle we had ever owned. I cared little that there would be no fishing as it was the furthest thing from my mind.

I was under the big truck with a flashlight in my teeth changing a gas bottle, disoriented because I was trying to compensate for being on my back envisioning which way to go with the left hand nut on the fitting when John Valentine pulled up. He stammers when excited.

After a few pre-season pleasantries he started: "Wwwwhen you get ssquared away, Frank, you ought to get up to the Rrrrrace 'cause they're getting a, a, a, lotta ... a, a, a, bbbbass!"

I crossed the threads on the connection, squirted LP into the moist air, fixed it, then yelled to Joyce to saddle up amid a tirade of complaints about dinner. We had to run the back track because the Traps had been cut away by the storm. Then, just as we were under the Race Light, the fog horn sounded, seeming to explode through our bones. Once we cleared the trail there to open beach, we could see that it was wall to wall buggies. Huge sweeps rolled around the corner from the east, the kind of water, when you are ankle deep, that can kill you. The wind carried the plugs deep into the humping Race, where lines tightened as soon as clutches were thrown. My plug drummed a few cycles before a bass clamped his maw down upon it. Looking left to see if Joyce knew that I was on, I could see her backing with a bowed rod.

Nice thing about early in the year is that there is no wondering if it might be a bluefish. Moreover, seasons never begin with 20-pound-plus fish in such numbers. Every caster there was either on or bent over with a knife. She and I collected roughly a box apiece and I knew that there would be no huge prices paid because Chesapeake watermen are flooding the market at this time.

Taking sellable numbers was a first for us that early in the season, but our experience has been that things tend to even off. But it wasn't going to even off that season.

Other commercials, people fishing the beach full time, continued throughout the month boxing fish nightly. Every June weekend paid off for us, but the last before coming out for the summer was murder.

Provincetown surf fishermen had gone into fishing the beach heavier than we had ever seen them. We had always fished with only a couple of townies but now there were four wheelers everywhere. Even some of the town regulars from Orleans, never before seen in P-Town, haunted the shore. While you could hit fish anywhere in the deep night, when traffic subsided, there were so many buggies plying the waterline trail, so many headlights on the water, that the real challenge was in finding some quiet water where the bass had not been flushed out—a place like the public swim beach.

That Friday night we slipped past the "No Vehicles Beyond This Point"

The morning after with me, Bob Bellmore and John Valentine. What nights they were.

sign without lights and worked a little point that I had never seen. There was a young kid there fishing. He didn't seem to be doing anything, so Joyce and I only planned to spend a few casts there, then scoot back out. I was a little uneasy about being in forbidden territory, what with old Ranger Rick ever a possibility.

It wasn't a big bar point and the water moved over it with only a slight increase in motion, but the linesides were stacked on the downtide edge. Joyce was on right away and I moved over to her spot while she followed her fish down. I had a take right away. But that kid never moved. I dragged both fish up without using a flashlight, put them away and we went down and did it again. Because we had moved so casually, it was not until maybe ten fish that the kid suspected that we might be catching fish.

"Hey mister, catching any?"

"A few. You?"

"Naw, nuthin' around. Hey, that lady got one."

I hooked up again without saying anything.

"You got one too? Jeez."

Joyce dragged up a 20ish, which the kid could see. "Jeez," he said.

Of course our company policy forbade helping anybody. The poor kid probably had 10 uncles. Moving to the side, out of the way, he started to cast with a will. Nothing. Every time one of us hooked up, I could hear him lamenting. That gosh-taked kid was ripping at me until I couldn't take it anymore.

"Hey kid, let me see your rig."

His plug was a sinker Rebel with hooks that looked as though they had been soaking in acid for a couple of years. Worse he had it clipped to 80 pound wire leader. Cutting it away, I tied one of our floaters that had a Red Gill up front. He talked and asked questions the whole time I set his gear right. Seeing him, Joyce came over and once she recognized that there was no problem, she greeted him. It took only a few minutes for her to recognize that he had a disability of some sort, an observation that already had begun to take hold with me. And she, always more partial to somebody with a handicap, walked him down to the point where the stripers lay, coached him into a short cast, and watched him hook up.

The fish moved off the same way that they always do, bending the Meade rod in his teen-aged hands, Joyce yelling "Set!" Poor bastard, trembling and uttering Jeez, followed. It wasn't bad enough that we had violated our all-abiding dictum of not helping anybody, but this was a townie and he was in serious danger of passing out. Still, he got his fish to shore, looked to be in the low thirties and he was beside himself with delight. We were shaking his hand and admiring it when someone came down this forbidden beach with his headlights on the water.

"How about shuttin' your effin' lights out!" ... my indulgence in being nice about things having run out. But instead of killing his headlights, the driver put on another: one of those blue gumball machines bolted to the top of the cab that goes in circles.

Walking up to the official vehicle, I quickly pointed out to the ranger that we didn't know that it was he, otherwise I would never have been guilty of such a gross indiscretion. Any other time I would have kept up the tirade in an effort to convince the officer how wrong he was with the hope that it would divert attention from what we had done. But it seemed to me at the time, what with all the stripers we had against the beach, that if there was ever a time to kiss his you-know-what it was now.

"There's too much traffic on the beach and it drives the bass hell west," I said, trying to sound as convincing, polite, and penitent as I could.

My dear beloved wife Joyce with the first 50 pounder she caught from a Cape beach.

"We saw this kid on when we were rounding the track and came down to help him out. Nice kid."

I hadn't gotten anywhere with the ranger until he saw Joyce backing in the quarter moonlight.

"Oh, the little lady has one on."

"Really? Wow, her first of the season. Jeez, that's great."

"Listen," the ranger said, "go ahead and enjoy yourselves, but I don't want you into this restricted area any deeper. Just go out the way you came when you're through."

Thanking him, I watched him slide back into the cab, his gun glistening, start the pickup, then swing a wide circle—headlights all over the shore. My ulcer and I sighed in unison as he bounded west.

The kid was packing up his pop bottle, bucket, and monster striper, out of his mind with joy, thanking "Mrs. Daignault," when he offered to return the Rebel and teaser rig. And she, placing her hand upon "Billy's" shoulder, told him that he could keep it, that we had many others. Between a good ranger and Billy, it was a time when I believed that the world had gone mad.

Where do you go on Saturday night when the traffic is heavier than it was the night before? Where do you go on Saturday night when you filled your boxes Friday night?

We expected Billy to be there and we expected to get thrown out ... this time. But maybe the District Ranger got wind that one of his men had shown a little discretion. Maybe the poor bastard lost his job for being human. Maybe they found a heart in him which caused him to flunk the physical for the Park Service. The only thing that resembled the night before was the fishing. Fact is that it was so good that we arranged to have Sunday night's load taken in Monday morning by one of the gang if, ahem, "We happened onto a few." We did. Same place.

Total for a two day weekend, that was stretched into Sunday night until 1:00 A.M. was 72 bass weighing 1200 pounds—$504. God help the poor sucker that chewed gum in Joyce's class the next day.

The way the season started and the way June went, I figured that we were bound for a letdown. True, there is no pattern, no guarantee, as to how the bass are going to run. Usually there is a run of big fish early July that might last 10 days or so. But the June fish were holding; we felt that we could identify them by their size as most were teen fish and a few in the low 20s. For the thousands caught, there had only been a pair of fifties—both by Pilgrims who knew little of the magnitude of their accomplishment. Each of these surfmen came back with all the friends that they could find. For a surfcaster, it was like dying and going to heaven. And when you are in heaven, I suppose, you may as well have your way with the place.

What was beginning to hit home was that few real kills were happening for the boatmen. Until '77 the boatmen did all the damage dragging jigs with wire line. The beach was merely a place where the entrenched traditions of casting rigged eels with squidders was practiced in this surfcaster's Mecca with far more resignation than success. We lost a lot of surf comrades who couldn't take the strain of watching the boatmen display their fish on the tailgate while running them to the dock, a gesture that no surfcaster with half a brain would venture. Stupid as it was for us to compete with them, each of us secretly wished for years that we could catch what they did. And most of them had given up the beach for what could be caught in boats.

Still, a few of us held out, clinging to the traditions, as though we suspected that there was a God in the heavens. Some of the boatmen admired us, perhaps because we personified the work ethic. Others looked upon us as stupid, perhaps because they had never caught any sellable number of striped bass until they went to boats. It was a rivalry that never enjoyed the upfrontmanship of so many others. We disliked their success, but never admitted it. They feared us, but never faced it. The delicious thing about the greatest blitz that the Striper Coast had ever seen was that we were, at long last, showing up the boatmen. I knew we were because we were seeing the boatmen fishing the beach again at night ... often as late as midnight.

What slackers they are. Three nights a week there would be a kill somewhere and the next night they would be there in their short boots casting badly for 15 minutes. How can a man's thumb remember its lessons when it has been tucked warmly in a pants pocket? Those idiots had been jerking their wire so long that they didn't know how to cast anymore.

There is an extra burst of energy that comes from knowing that the fish are somewhere. We had a series of good nights at the Race that everybody knew about, then the bass left and had to be found. Joyce and I went east to the back beach and found them by working each point at various stages of the tide, always alone. Come daybreak, a few of the dawn patrol would find us and the fish. Some nights the New York crowd was around but they always kept their distance. We would see them at the dock unloading the next day. Mid-July was not murder but steady. Virtually all the bass were between 30 and 45 pounds. Poor Joyce was kicking the tires, however, because she could not land a fish that cleared the 40 mark. When I met her at 16 she was catching itty-bitty smallmouths in Spring Lake with her father, in a boat. Now she was on the world's finest striper beach lamenting 38 pounders as though they were sunnies stealing her crawdad. Some women.

She came out of it on a week night at the Mission Bell. A moderate sou'west was coming over the dunes, nice conditions. We had pulled up and spread, her to the east. We had a few in the box but no big slaughter or the girls would have been with us. The fish were there so I didn't move the buggy. I had seen her go back to the rig slowly and knew she had taken something. I had one on the shore and had felt a couple of nudges. During a lull, I went down to her and she said she had one up top. After I brought my fish up I went around to the front to stow it, lest somebody come by and see it. No lights, but I could make out its form and it was a moose. Anxiously, I spread my hands for its length, a set of hands being 16 inches, the legal length of bass at the time. Her fish was three sets of hands plus about four inches—over 50.

There had been a letter from Dickie that he was taking leave between his tour on the *Hamilton* and his next duty station at Kodiak. We called home that morning and delighted in hearing his voice again. He thrilled at word that Mom had taken a 50 pounder and I urged him to come down because of the fishing.

That night he was on the beach with us for the first time in two years, reminiscing about the years before, asking about Nauset. It was the first time the place had even crossed my mind that season.

CHAPTER 17

Best of Times

Dickie arrived in P-Town at the best possible time. Tides were low in the Race at midnight, a stage when we had always done a job. We had a big dinner on the beach, laying plans for the upcoming night. Joyce was cleaning up with the girls when I hauled a box from England out from under the bunks. It was the care package that Alex Ingram had sent me when I raved to him in a letter saying just how good his Red Gills were. The boy gasped when he saw the 75 teasers, brand new in their packages. As I taught him how to set them ahead of the plug on the leader, I explained that we had never had anything that brought the stripers to the hook better. What was important here was that no one else had any; these were the only Red Gills in North America.

Sunset we worked the Back Beach east through the falling tide. Every point held a number of buggies and there were a few bass laying on the beach. The six of us felt good about all being together again, but I was mildly distracted with the thought that if these greenies were putting fish on the beach, what would it be like when my killers went to work with the rubber jobs from England? We settled on the last point before the Mission Bell where Vince and another were fishing. There were no fish on the shore, but I new that meant nothing.

Sandra set on a fish right off. True to what he had done when they were younger, Dickie went to her right away. I scolded him, pointing out that she could handle it, then stuffed his old surf rod into his hands. I think Vince thought that he had been invaded. Having come out earlier, he had no idea how many other fishermen were on the beach.

We were all hauling on stripers, which to Valentine looked good enough when he was coming down the beach. No doubt the casters at the uptide point could still see well enough to know that we were hot, causing them to move east to our point. Within minutes the place was so crowded that I whistled everybody in and we bounded east to the next point. More bass, but now it was full dark and we never used a light to unhook or stow fish.

Around 10:30 I collected Dickie and one of his sisters who had wandered east and we headed for the Race. Passing what buggies that remained, we could see that things had slowed. Dickie had a 47 pounder and a couple of others, but the big one was larger than any he had ever caught. The night was young.

Dropping the girls at the big buggy, Mom stayed with us for the low water fishing. The Race was ghostlike, empty of casters, when we dropped down onto the bar, sliding softly, me watching the vehicle's shadow to gauge our distance from the water. The three of us spread without a word. The light made its rhythmic pass exposing a dorsal two rod lengths from my boots.

"Dad!"

"I know, I know, keep casting."

Stripers, big stripers. Spread along the shallow surf in single numbers here and there, we could see dorsals or tails as they rooted in the bottom for sand eels. My plug had passed a dozen of them as I worked north trying to find one that would take. Joyce and Dickie were at the buggy and I knew that they were talking of the frustration of having such big fish so close. Dickie went down with a clean, leaderless five inch swimmer—a thing that had so often worked when we found picky fish. Nothing.

Valentine came out of the thin fog to join us.

"Hhhey, Frank, what's with these fffoolish fffish?"

"I don't know, John, they have their moods."

It was like a bad dream. Sixty, eighty cents a pound, freaking gold mine. We had a 100 years of surfcasting experience between us, a ton of money in tackle, duty free Red Gills panting for a shot at them, and it was all junk.

I forget the time, but a good part of the night was gone when it occurred to me to cast a fly. The nine foot salmon rod was always on the roof rack of the buggy in case we ran into a bunch of schoolies that wanted something small. It wasn't the right tackle for these moby fish, but what could I lose? I felt a little stupid bringing it down, but it was a card that could be played in the face of certain defeat. A tail rolled first this way then that, as it sought to balance upon its chin in the shallows. The fly passed without incident. Next cast I let it settle, waiting longer than a side of me wanted to. Stripping line in short jerks past where I thought its head and my fly might be, everything stopped as though I had hooked a stump. Then the brute continued feeding as though my offer had been just one more bauble of cuisine.

Stepping back, I drove the rod tip over my shoulder, but only the butt end came back, the tip bowing to the weight of the fish. There was a pause, as though it sought to decipher its predicament, then it went. Fly line shot through the guides so fast that I was into the backing within seconds. The boy and I chased for ten minutes while I put line back on the spool of the single action reel, desperately trying to wind it on as quickly as it was available. It would spin, then stop, and I would crank. There was 200 feet of line out when the monster flailed the surf down the shore to my left. Dickie ran and gaffed it.

Retying the fly, I found another. Allowing the fly to settle, I slowed the retrieve, felt the take without movement, and drove the steel. This striper's movement was deeper into the Race, which had started to rise on the outside, the forces greater as the fish gained speed in the current. The drag moved more grudgingly now as line depleted, forcing me to walk deeper toward the fish as I unscrewed tension from the drag. Then the reel seemed to rebel against the striper's run, stalling when the bass stopped, requiring greater force to get it going. Once it began to spin, it would do so too easily, yielding line too cheaply. In no time I was down at the bottom of the backing with no sign of making any headway. If I tightened, the reel would give no line; when I backed off, the reel spun so rapidly that coils of braid lifted and crossed one another. Then, with 20 yards left, the line backlashed, lifted momentarily from the water, then cut itself at the reel.

It was one of the most sickening sunrises that I had ever experienced. A hundred monster stripers fed in the wash of Race Point to the astonishment of the best surfcasters in the world. But only I knew how to take them and the means for doing it were gone, my salmon rod dead without a fly line. I had a 43 pound striper that had been dwarfed by the one that cleaned me.

Late that morning, after three hours sleep, I unloaded at the dock before going to Orleans for a salmon reel. One does not shop for a salmon reel on Cape Cod without raising eyebrows, but I did find one that had a nylon drag system with rim control. At the beach I spliced a new number 10 rocket taper to some fresh braid; then I attached a home tapered leader that went down in three sections from 40 pound to 20. I was loaded for bear and felt better about going to sleep late that afternoon.

Driving east that evening, they all chattered about the night's possibilities, but I could not talk to them. Something was happening to time; something was happening to the order of things. I was beginning to see that having one of them come back, for so short a time, only elevated the pain of having one gone. These were no longer babies and lives of their own were taking shape. You could escape to Cape Cod but you could not run away from time. Two, maybe three nights, and Dickie would be gone. Thoughts of it all saddened and distracted me from the business at hand.

The buggies were positioned on the Back Beach the same way they had been the night before, but few were fishing. This was a bad sign, clear indication that nothing was being taken, not even after the tide matched the night before, well after dark. Watching the west, I saw the headlights of buggies leaving for town. Hitless, I drove the girls back to the big truck, Mom turning in herself, weary. The boy and I killed some time to let the Race down, joining the girls as they filled up on chips and pop. I could tell that he was thinking of old times, that there were not many nights left, as he smooched them each their turn before we left for the Race.

My heart wasn't in it as I mechanically cast the fly to each brute striper that showed itself in the shallows. One by one, they took the feathers, eight in all, to 40 pounds. I horsed them with the heavy tippet and Dickie wrestled them in the wash until dawn. The others just watched. They knew that it was pointless. By full brightness the fish moved off and the buggies left the Race.

The boats had not done much that season, but the following day they did nothing. At the dock there were a few boxes from Billingsgate but virtually nothing from local waters. The great blitz of '77 seemed to have ended.

Dickie was badly in need of rest and he had not seen many of his old friends. With all the kids taking a night off, Joyce and I worked east from the Mission Bell. Nothing. I dropped her off after midnight, checked the Race. Nothing.

Next day when we took the boy to town to say goodbye, I handed him over a month's Coast Guard pay, his share of the take for those few nights of surfcasting. Joyce didn't sob openly, but the tears just flowed down her cheeks. Though I thought I was doing a good job of hiding it, my mouth twisted uncontrollably and they both knew that the tears were in my heart. As his small used car drifted out of sight down Route 6, I felt the same loneliness, the same sense of accelerating time.

Six weeks of night on night surfcasting had taken a toll. The girls expressed no interest and Joyce was haggard. Instead of fishing we feasted on lobster bought from one of the beach fishermen, then drank cold wine and slept in the dark—something I had not yet done that season.

There is an out-of-step feeling that comes from missing a night. Still, there was no one to chide us about something we might have missed. At the dock, there were a few bluefish slips, clear evidence that the show was over. Again we fished east until we got to the red gunk at High Head, routinely checking the Race before turning in, earlier each night. A week went by without a drop of fish for us. Not that we needed it; I had been depositing so many healthy checks at the bank that we could have stayed until Christmas cod were running if we had to. But with all the rest, and the memory of what we had so fresh in mind, I hungered for a new challenge, another blitz. The bass couldn't be gone. For the first time the price went over one dollar per pound.

I pored over the log trying to find some indication that there was something we had learned another season that might hint at some new direction. I searched the maps: Jeremy Point, out of bounds, but navigable in the deep night. This turned out to be a scary drive without headlights, we so distracted that we were barely able to fish. Then I remembered a conversation with Paulie the year before about fishing way east. He had said that

We found monsters in the Race surf that could only be taken with the fly. My best was this 43 pounder but there was another that made off with all my fly line.

the red gunk cleaned up if you drove far enough east. If the westerlies held, Highland Light was as pure as a bathtub. That afternoon we dressed like tourists and walked the grounds of the Coast Guard Station there, gasping at the height above the sea and the purity of the view through a gunkless, emerald sea. Then we drove in both directions, marking access places where there were breaks in the dunes as far south as Newcomb Hollow.

Our first night east was a full blown expedition complete with a lunch, cold drinks, and rigged eels. Sunset we shifted into four just above the lighthouse, dropping precariously downhill before turning southeast. Only a half mile over sand and we had to turn back at a place where the surf washed a 200 foot cliff. South, we went on at Balston Beach with all the same fears. Here, however, the drop was less for the buggy, but our care with the headlights had nearly caused us to drive off a six foot washout. I really had the horrors because there was something strange and forboding about this country. There was a closed in feeling, a feeling of being unable to escape the sea. The dunes towered over us, blocking out the moonlight, casting shadows upon the surf. Bars ran perpendicular to the beach, leaving holes between them, edges frothing from the breaking waves. It was more like Nauset both in the movement of the sea and the texture of the sand. Yet here there was little evidence of other surfmen, if any. One set of tracks led the way—probably the ranger patrol.

After determining just how close we could get to Highland Light, my best reference for positioning ourselves, we backtracked to a nice hole and shut down. Here Joyce and I made a few casts, then practically ran back to the buggy, totally spooked. She sat in the buggy and I poured some coffee from the thermos.

"Scary."

"Sure is."

"There's no need for it."

"I know. Still scary."

"Let's try."

The eel hit a section of foam then passed into a dark section where the bar gave way to deeper water. It pulsed from the rhythm of my retrieve as a striper changed direction. Then the fish accelerated behind the eel, lunged, then felt the steel of the 9/0 siwash. God, I love to fish.

The place was so new to us that we had no names for the specific locations that we fished. We assigned some and that first hole was called "Forty Pound." At the "Foraxe" Joyce had her eel batted and landed a lineside in the thirties a few minutes later. I think we might have gotten more fish that first night at Balston, but the rising tide erased the definition of the bars.

On the second night, what with the additional hour before the tide was at the same level, we landed five with nothing under 30 pounds. Now we had names for every fishable hole from Newcomb to Highland: Point Nine Mile, Indian, Scary Narrows—the latter named for the only section of beach that still kept us uneasy. On the third night, I made it a point to watch how late into the tide we could cross at Scary without driving into water. That is one of the things about this kind of surf fishing. It is not only what is caught, but what is learned. We had enough good holes to keep us going well into the night. Up to now, the tide had controlled how much time we had. But adding an hour to our available time each night, we would need more holes. If what we were using was a sound basis for judging all of it, the mile between Scary Narrows and Highland Light had to have as good a set of holes as the rest; and, that mile would be needed.

Our most definitive view of the area came at sunset of the fifth night.

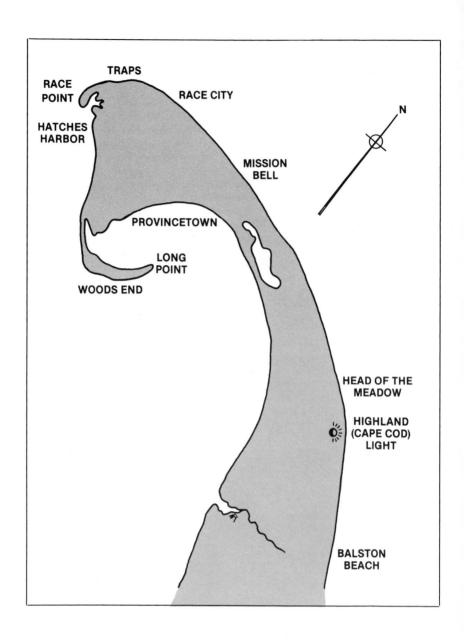

TRAPS

RACE POINT

RACE CITY

HATCHES HARBOR

N

MISSION BELL

PROVINCETOWN

LONG POINT

WOODS END

HEAD OF THE MEADOW

HIGHLAND (CAPE COD) LIGHT

BALSTON BEACH

With the tide out we could see that each bar ran roughly perpendicular to the shore hooking nor'west at its end. Where the bar met the beach, there was always a deep dark hole where sand eels collected. We dropped the buggy down to low beach past Scary, scooted to the top, and rounded a curve under the lighthouse within minutes. I could clearly see the impassable spot that had stopped us the first night. Our knowledge of the shore in this strange, forboding Outer Cape beach was complete.

Once it was full dark, we started work in front of Highland and Joyce stuck a fish within minutes. I crowded her to be certain that there were no others, and we moved to the next hole. She picked up another, again on the nor'west side, which made me suspect that the bass were feeding more on the left sides of the bars than the rights where I was fishing. I gaffed her second, made a cast, and hooked one of my own. At close to 300 pounds, water now rushing over the bars so deep that we both fished from the slant beach, I remembered that Scary Narrows would be tight by now and called to Joyce to leave.

It was the first time in a couple of nights that I had again gotten uneasy. Pulling the switch out on the headlights, I gunned the buggy until we got there. Foam was sliding right to the dune base, then it would all fall back down exposing the sand. I timed the movement of the surf. The fourth wave always seemed to be a biggie and the second the smallest. Between the second foamer and the third we scooted down the hill toward the water, I paused on the accelerator, watched the sea slide backward, and gunned the buggy through to the dry sand on the other side.

The buggie's headlights went across the sand cliffs ahead, swung left over the surf, exposed the washout then compelled me for another try. This time I accelerated toward a number four, fully knowing that it was spent, and the rig leaped toward the water as it slid out of our way as if to acknowledge that I had tamed our one remaining fear at Balston Beach.

Joyce was bitching her brains out at my foolishnss. I paid no attention to her, swung around, and we drove out again just ahead of a four that clawed to catch up with us. With safe beach exit ahead of us, we could still read the bar holes well enough to top off the boxes at 500 pounds.

Next day we dropped the iced fish late in the afternoon to avoid detection; the beach crowd always brought theirs mornings. But, from what the slips illustrated, there were few people coming to the dock. We needed only avoid some stray boatman scrounging ice for his beer cooler. The girls were psyched, conscious that summer was ending, that they could salt some good bonus money, now that we had some bass on the go again. Carol stayed behind because she loved having the big buggy to herself.

All sense of forboding was gone when we ghosted through the access at Balston. I felt so comfortable there that I dropped the rig to low beach, loafing the engine comfortably clear to the lighthouse where I swung around to a darling hole to drop Susan. Her sister listened to the instructions, knowing that for her they would be the same. Then, Sandra stepped off the tailgate on the next stop without a word. It was unconscious, but we all whispered, as though in keeping with our subtle movements. No radio, no headlights, we were mere shadows leaving lines in the wet sand that the next tide would wash clean. I was easing off for Joyce's stop when the short flash of one of them caught my rear mirror.

"One of them signaled! Try it here."

Joyce's rod cleared the bumper spike quickly, she knowing that I had to get back. I passed Sandra at high speed, she pointing to her left. On the bar, Sue was backing, her feminine form silhouetted clearly. At her fore the sea

With a wife taking fish like these you can be a highliner by just being a good coach.

exploded from a wild, thrashing striper that sought desperately to exert destructive forces upon her equipment. Then a small wave broke and it trapped itself in the shallows where I slid the gaff into its gill covers. Just as my knife lanced the Rebel clear, Susan saw her sister's signal—one, lone, flick of the light. The 40 odd pounder hit the bottom of the box with a thump and I was gunning the rig within seconds. Whipping the family car along the waterline, I saw another flash and cursed to myself at Sandy's carelessness for signaling twice when I realized that I was much closer to her. As I approached, I could see the form of a large striper on the dry sand, her rod laying on her sweater 20 feet from it. When I pulled up, Sandy lifted one of the surfrods up front urging me to help Mom.

By the time I got to Joyce, she was against the dune base, 200 feet from the water, her line straining on a brute that was close to 50, just cruising in the wash. It seemed perplexed and tired, oblivious to my movements behind it. After it was beached, I raised my arm to signal Joyce. I was bending over it when she asked about the girls.

"This is going to be some kind of freakin' night!"

Back to the nor'west.

As I approached Sandra, her rod was bent, but she urged me to tend to Sue because, as Sandy lamented:

"Her light went on a long time ago."

The whole thing was so crazy that it was no longer a case of helping one of them, but rather, a question of determining who was closest to stalling out because of equipment needs. It was clear to me that they were too far apart. Joyce and the girls were spread a half mile, Sandra was running out of clothes, and I was running out of surfrods. There were only two bass in the buggy, but there was another 100 pounds on the beach and more than that on the lines. I wasn't seeing signals because most of my time was spent tending hooks. Even when I urged Susan to get in the buggy, her voice cracked, begging me to let her stay.

"Dad, they are popping all over the place. I should stay here."

Looking to my left, I could see the dark stains that the swirls made as bass turned to inhale the sand eels.

When I passed Sandra, she was idle, two fish on the beach. Mom was waiting with another. Nobody wanted to give up their spot. Mom and Sandra jumped into the vehicle reluctantly, but their trepidation vanished once I told them that Susan and I could see the fish. I could have lived with a few less striped bass.

That year we had some good summer fishing from Newcomb Hollow to Highland Light.

CHAPTER 18

The Magic

That night at Balston Beach Joyce and the twins hauled just under 900 pounds. Nothing in the load was under 30 pounds in weight and most were in the mid-forties. When it ended, Susan and Sandra lifted their bare feet toward the tailgate to avoid a wash that strained to catch us as we scooted through Scary Narrows. I never made a cast in what was to be the biggest surfcasting night our family had ever known. Some would say that we could have done better if I had taught them to remove fish themselves. But removing a plug with nine barbs from a thrashing bull striper is no doubt the most dangerous thing that a surfcaster does. Having a hook in your hand is one thing; having 40 pounds of live striper on the other end of that hook carves your predicament in stone.

Then there is the teaser, three or four feet up from the plug. It is so easy, when looking at a big fish with your plug in his mouth, to forget the teaser hook, bend to remove the plug and drive it into your face. When the excitement of battle is in place, so much can be forgotten at the very time when all is supposed to be remembered. Surfcasting is like any other profession: If you don't know what you are doing, it can cost you. How much are you going to catch when sitting in an accident room 50 miles from where stripers are?

I love them all too much to have them hurt. I love having them beside me too much to risk one incident that might have them thinking twice before some other night of surfcasting. For me it has always been as great a thrill to see my charges hook up as it was to hook up myself.

We lost nothing by having me out of the water, because my service—passing a rod, cutting out a plug—had to be done by somebody. I could have hooked them no quicker than any of those three. And none of them could have hefted fish of that size into the boxes.

Next night I was gillie for them again and it was a carbon copy with 100 less in poundage. There was so much striped bass to be hidden from the beach community at Race City that we hid them in a friend's barn in town for the late afternoon drops that avoided detection. I know that it bothered some people that we always came in so early in the morning from fishing when it was so bad. But it was never known by the right ones, the ones who were beginning to wonder about the absence of fish slips at the dock. The drop for that August week's check was 2300 pounds, priced at exactly $1.00 per pound. Another week like that would have paid for our new buggy, which, by the way, didn't smell new anymore.

But the great blitz of '77 had a dark side. Except for Conrad and George DeRosa, we had never had townies on the beach before. With all the fish on the beach, prices climbing, the locals snapped up every four wheel drive that would run. People who heard about the blitz came from inland. Many were friends of those who had been coming for years. Word of the Race's productivity was universal. Where we had once fished it alone, daring to call it 'our yard,' it was often difficult to park on all but the windiest nights.

Some days, afternoons when the sou'west blew into the window above my bunk, I thought about where it was all going. We seemed to be passing through an endless parade of fortune and decline. Just when we had a hotspot figured, a regulation, or discovery by the throngs, would take it away. First Chatham Inlet, then Race Point. Always, we had been able to

The good fishing of the Great Blitz brought townies out onto the beach, most of whom had never been seen fishing before.

cover the loss with a new discovery. Now it was Balston/Highland Light. How long before someone coming out of a restaurant, not even fishing, might see one bass tail that had been neglectfully exposed to full view as our buggy passed? Nothing stays a secret. When it happens, where next? You can't go any further east when you are on Cape Cod.

I knew that the blitz was a major event in surfcasting when it was happening. This is not one of those good-old-days things that comes to mind as an afterthought. Nobody had ever cast a fishing line into such great shoals of striped bass. And what were the experts telling us when this was happening? They were saying that we were running out of stripers. They lamented; they preached; they raised money; they told the people who wrote the stories about fishing that there were no more stripers. What were those checks piled on my bureau until Christmas that I was afraid to cash because the IRS would wonder where a pair of teachers got the money, a dream?

Moreover, it was the same song that had become popular in 1970. Then, they told us the bass were in decline when the Chesapeake had just finished the finest decade of reproduction it had ever known. Everywhere that I fished for stripers, from Fisher's Island to the Merrimack, you could find them in the deep night and be by yourself. Yet, the next day you would pick up the paper and find some columnist lamenting the loss of the fish. I knew who they were, having talked to many of them at writer conventions, and they had never—with certain exceptions—even fished for striped bass. Decline was the thing to write about. In all my years on the Striper Coast, I always found the fishing better than what was being said. Truth is that there was much more talking going on than fishing, but it would be too great a digression from the mission of this to carry this discussion any further.

A year after the blitz I wrote an article in *Salt Water Sportsman* magazine that editor, Frank Woolner, hesitated to print. Once he checked on it, however, he found support from his spies, as he called them, and went ahead. Of course the Boston paper, with their weekly fishing reports, had never made mention of the good fishing in P-Town which caused readers, who relied upon these reports, to complain bitterly. One outdoor editor sought to discredit the article, but found a picture of Joyce with a pair of 40 pounders to be authentic because our 1977 beach permit was in view. I can't believe that it only takes a pair of 40 pounders to establish credibility. You could have such fish even if the fishing were as bad as they said. Of course such fishing reports, in this case based upon contacts on Cape Cod, were also in question. I can make no statement either way as to whether the "reporters" kept quiet, or genuinely did not know. It might have been a little of both. However, the doubt on the part of some was laid to rest and the sense of disquiet a writer suffers when he is not believed subsided.

The dock taught me a curious lesson late that year. I was making a drop sometime during the week after the big one. Nothing unusual, routine, a few fish, I don't recall. When I hopped up on the shipping platform I was struck by the sight of dozens of shiny, new snow shovels—something we had never seen before. A few lumpers were scurrying around, but most were slacking—smoking cigarettes and practicing their vulgarity, one peeing down a drain spout. Then I realized that the floor was awash in lobsters, creeping along like farmyard pets, one having just dropped off the edge into Provincetown Harbor. We are not talking a few boxes here. There were cages of them, thousands of pounds, all alive. What I could see so clearly was the spill off from what was being weighed, the escapees. The lumper would shovel a bunch onto the scale and a few would drop to the floor, some creeping off undetected to find cover among the broken fish boxes or

The truth about the blitz was that, for the first time, the truly great fishing was for surfcasters.

The blitz went unreported until my article came out in *Salt Water Sportsman* in 1978. Even with a year I had scooped the world reporting on it. The sticker on the buggy's bumper (left end, above spinning reel) when examined with a jeweler's loupe, proved to outdoor reporters that we had the year right.

among the aisles of boxed fish dripping ice water. When I called Joyce in to see it, she giggled and gasped at the same time. Always, I had felt, that I had a mind for counting the boxes, figuring the pounds of what was there quickly. It was a game I played, multiplying, trying to measure how many people would eat fish in Philadelphia or New York because of what was there. But here, now, all sense of numbers, pounds, or dollars, became a jumble of value. You just had to accept it as being both awesome and funny.

In the office the stogie smoke had stratafied over the trawler skipper who sat patiently waiting for his receipt. He perspired, breathed heavily, seemed lost in thought, unable or unwilling to recognize me.

"Hey, Cappy," I said, "who belongs to all them animals out there?"

His eyes recognized me though he didn't want to; his grin told me the lobsters were his though he did not want to swagger.

"Cappy, what the hell kind of money we talkin' about here?"

The acrid smoke rolled out from under his graying mustache, he leaned back, perhaps to give me time to remember when he had said so many years before that I was making good money for fishing the beach, and said:

" 'Bout eleven grand."

Looking through the glass enclosure, I tried to fathom how much lobster was out there, what it was like to have the strain gauge tell you that your net was full of money fish. I pictured the despair of one bad day fishing, against the drama of when it was good, when he said, "The magic comes, the magic goes."

For us that year the magic was 11,500 pounds of striped bass that brought in $7500 after the kids all had theirs. There were some teachers in Massachusetts working all year to earn that.

CHAPTER 19

The Hunt

We had no right to expect another spring like the last, though some foolishly expected it. Instead, a stray bass came in from the Race or there would be a small kill at Wood End. Later in June, the Billingsgate Shoals gave up some fish as they had since the beginning of sport fishing.

Our first week of summer produced a small load one night at the Race which I ended up wishing we had never taken because it built a false hope that kept us in P-Town too long. Balston was completely out of character giving up nothing for three nights. All that was left were evening tides building at Nauset which would give us a good shot during the week.

Strange how, when you've been away from a place for a year, how different it feels. There were a few short buggies at the Inlet with younger men whom I did not know. By 10:00 they were all gone, their lights bounding north when Joyce connected first—a bass in the twenties. We beached a few more at slack tide, then worked on a heavy concentration of picky fish that were taking up positions in the current during the drop. It was very much the same as it had been during the earlier years; maybe there were less schoolies. By low tide on the chart, a time when the inlet was flying, a buggy with a New York plate pulled up without talking to us.

Not that that surprised me, because all of them that I had known stayed pretty much to themselves unless they were trying to get information. This guy needed no refresher course on what was happening because his movements were too deliberate. He seemed to know too well where he was supposed to be, and how he was supposed to work it. But that didn't bother me as much as the fact that we had never seen a New Yorker on Nauset Beach before. It was one of those inevitabilities that everyone seemed to fear because all knew that it was only a matter of time before the P-Town crowd, which meant New Yorkers, would turn to Nauset when things went badly there. We left near dawn and I saw his buggy behind us on low beach as we hustled the 11 miles at 40 miles per hour. When he passed us on the highway, we could see the Red Gills trailing from his rods. Our secret was out.

Our drop was seen next day by a few people we did not know. I couldn't shake the feeling that we were recognized. That night on Nauset there were three license plates from the city, one of the rigs with four fishermen. Once darkness set in I could tell that they were taking bass at about the same rate as we. But these guys were sharp, never putting on a light and making sure that they left no fish on the beach to be discovered by someone coming in. Joyce and I happened to hook up at the same time drawing three of them to both sides of us. After loading the two fish we left without incident because I was sure that we could do as well behind Long Bar ... alone.

Always on these beaches we kept private sets of landmarks which we named so that we could be specific in conversation and use them to find exact locations on moonless nights or when fog so shrouded the seascape that all the shore looked the same. South of where Long Bar meets the shore there was a point where the currents accelerated, where the bass would often pause as they cruised the beach. On that point, well above the high tide mark, there was a scraggy, tattered bush perhaps cast adrift from some distant island or washed down from some river in spate. It was the only thing that set that piece of shore apart and it became namesake for Bush

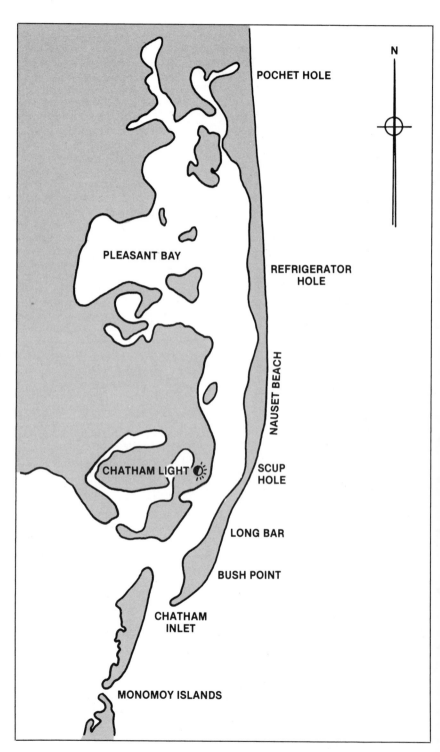

N

POCHET HOLE

REFRIGERATOR
HOLE

PLEASANT BAY

NAUSET BEACH

CHATHAM LIGHT

SCUP
HOLE

LONG BAR

BUSH POINT

CHATHAM
INLET

MONOMOY ISLANDS

Point. With the help of it, we matched the previous night's catch. But the tides were getting late for Nauset and I knew that as the dark moon approached—high tide at midnight—that our catch would drop off. These would not be suitable water levels for the Race either, in spite of the fact that we had given the place a few nights to improve. It was a case of having other options open once Nauset fell off, and it did. Joyce had one lineside in the forties our last night so we followed up with a probe of the bars and holes at Balston/Highland Light before high water forced us off.

That weekend, a time when I always find solace in not having anything in particular on the go, we watched the sunset at Race Point, boatmen jigging in vain, then worked the Back Beach without a touch. Saturday morning, I picked up the same stale fish check twice, though I had nothing to drop, used the lumper's latrine, packed ice slowly, hung around the dock until the Wharfinger asked me to move my rig, hoping for a shread of evidence that somebody was doing something somewhere. I learned they were catching 12 cent bluefish.

Sunday night, early morning tides, nobody around, we went back to Nauset, confident that we were missing nothing to the north. We were cruising the waterline trail under a faltering sun when Joyce spotted a bass on the surface spitting distance from the beach and took it. With no water at the inlet, we shut down until full darkness at this spot and proceeded to take three boxes. Near sunrise when we left, we were astounded to find several buggies spread along the beach and not a solitary surfcaster was asleep. We had not been alone.

With all our years at Nauset, we had done little serious fishing along the beach, except for Pochet Hole. But that season it was the desolate barrier beach of Nauset that saved us when the tides were wrong for the inlet. Moreover, the 10 miles there provided enough suitable fishing water to allay all danger of ever having to work any hole in a crowd. For instance, there was a washout just above the Old Harbor Coast Guard Station where the trail cut to the back providing a three quarter mile stretch of shore that was not driven and could not be seen by anyone passing. We would pass it, then cut back north past a barrier erected by the police, tucking the buggy against the dunes. Here we could fish the shore without ever bringing attention to the place by our presence.

Always, when there is a washout on the beach, that change in topography extends below the surface. Up top, the dunes were cut away and eroding from spring tides. Where a hole between two high dunes showed obvious vulnerability, cottage owners had piled some driftwood pallets and a cast out refrigerator, hoping to hold back the sea. Below the surface, the depth could be read as emerald calm by day, black and foamless by night. Bars flanked the two edges, making right angle turns to the beach. At the corners the waves clapped together, but along the inside of the bars that came to the beach, the foam would die out marking the deep water perfectly. I remember feeling an inner excitement each time we dropped the buggy against the surf to pass the police barrier. This nightly tinge of excitement was not without basis. It was, after all, the "Refrigerator Hole" that kept body and soul together for both of us that season.

More than half the bass we took in '78 came from Refrigerator Hole but the biggest night was in early August. We found the fish there low in a rising tide just after sunset. At first we had each taken a bar corner but the action that Joyce was getting interrupted me so often that I stayed with her. Both of us cast Rebels with Red Gill teasers beaching fish that were mostly over 40 pounds. When action slowed to an occasional contact, we went to rigged

More than half the bass we took in '78 came from the Refrigerator Hole. The best night was in early August.

eels and the hits came as though no one had fished there yet. Then, when the eels slowed down, we went to the plugs and droppers and started all over again.

One of my fish had made so violent a run on my heavy rig, one with 45-pound braid, that I was certain that I was fighting the World Record. One thinks that way when wrestling 45 pounders effortlessly. This lineside had run me down to the bottom of the spool when Joyce came down with the gaff. Fortunately, nothing broke when I clamped down on the reel. Then, after a few minutes of serious horsing, I beached a 53-pounder with the treble hook of my plug in its vent.

During the last hour of darkness, our hookups had fallen off considerably, though we still drew repeated bats and swipes. We were exhausted, maybe 15 stripers in the buggy and close to that spread about the shore. We had easily dropped or rolled as many fish as we had caught, plus all those that had taken short, which prompted me to think that every fish in the hole had encountered our offers at some point during the night. I called Joyce from the water, knowing that she was exhausted:

"Take a break, we've stuck just about everything that is here."

Whereupon, I rinsed and packed all the remaining fish lest some interloper pass upon low beach at daybreak and see our take. Joyce smudged all the drag marks with foot prints, and we poured stale coffee from vacuum bottles as the first fire of another day smoldered to the east.

Darkness lingered, but there was enough light to make out the horizon, enough to question what one sees. Three casts out there were a few disturbances that caught my attention; Joyce could see that I was looking at something. Then, as the horizon fell into focus, as our view of the seascape matured, we could see a quarter-mile width of striped bass porpoising wildly upon a placid sea for a mile in each direction. We distinctly had not stuck them all.

But I should have known, when I examined the figures for the season, that the storm clouds were on the horizon. Our money take for the year was the same as the one before. Yet our *catch* was down 40 percent. Bass prices were increasing faster than inflation. The perennial call from conservationists for a no-sell law lacked integrity because it was both doomed by bad timing and suffered the weakness of coming from the same people who told us that the bass was dwindling in 1970 after the best decade of reproduction ever known. We had heard too much from them when things were good.

Then there was the curse of measurement. Things were always changing in our operation. How could we measure the success of one season against that of another? Just when we had a spot figured, learned how to take bass from it, regulation would interfere. Or, so many other fishermen went to it that we had to move on. It was a social and legal treadmill that kept us ever running at a faster pace to box more stripers for higher prices. There was no measurement for the effort that we put forth in the endless mid-watch hunts for stripers, always compensating for our own dwindling family.

Dickie was in Alaska; our little housekeeper, Carol, had met a boy and run off to California. The way things were going, I was going to catch all these stripers myself.

That season it was the desolate barrier beach of Nauset that saved us when the tides were wrong at the inlet.

CHAPTER 20

Where Are the Bass?

1979. For the first time in a long time I was alone with my bride. It was a time that we had awaited for 23 years. The big truck seemed luxurious for the space it provided two of us. Now, we could drive off at sunset in the chase vehicle to fish any stretch of the Outer Cape from the Race to Chatham Inlet.

Normally, late June is a time when Cape stripers can be found anywhere, but not that season. Race Point was awash with surfcasters, their buggies parked so close that they blocked out the flash of Race Light. Men quarrelled over space to spike their surfrods while they waited for fish to pass the beach and take the fresh sand eels set to the bottom. To us it was a sickening sight to have the spot we had fished alone less than 20 years before taken from us in this way. But surfcasting was no longer the game we had known; now, men slumped over their steering wheels asleep with up to four baited rods each until an unsuspecting lineside took one down. The rods were guarded around the clock without regard for conditions. No longer was it a case of fighting a wind with a plug, conditions bad enough to drive away the regulars that once fished there. The old traditions of working the beach had been replaced with waiting; the old guard were so outnumbered by bait men that they were difficult to find.

We tried all the spots: Mission Bell, Highland Light, Balston, Nauset Inlet, Pochet, the Refrigerator Hole, Bush Point, Chatham Inlet. Most often it was for nothing. Now and then we took a pair of linesides from a small concentration of fish, but it was at best a slow pick. The price rose to two dollars per pound, but there was nothing. Word circulated at times that it had gone over three, but it could have been $10 because ten dollars times nothing is still nothing.

Mid-July we had to leave the beach to visit Susan on her first liberty from the Coast Guard Academy. We were awed by the razor edge organization and intimidating prominence of so fine an institution until we saw our baby. "Youngies" formed up at attention, braced at a level that to us seemed painful until Susan came down to be inspected by an upper classman. She seemed so slight, so out-of-place, having lost ten pounds from when she was fitted with her first dress blues. Joyce and I cried.

Her twin, Sandra, was like a fish out of water that summer. Weeks shy of 18, Sandy perspired her last summer away beside the ovens of an inland pizza parlor before entrance at Massachusetts Maritime Academy. It was her first and last summer without the Atlantic.

Vast stretches of the Outer Cape had become a wasteland that was devoid of all surfcasters. By August, any evidence of stripers went under close scrutiny. I even went after a school of bluefish in the Second Rip one morning, just for an excuse to peruse the dock. That day I found a 40-pound-plus striper on the scale with a trace of sand that had escaped a careful rinse. From the texture of the gravel I could tell that it had been taken between Newcomb and the Highlands. That night we saw a buggy there and worked every hole on the beach for a lone fish that went for $100.

Maybe the real money in stripers was speculating about where they had gone. One magazine author said that the rod and reel commercials had killed them all. Another said the pollution in the Chesapeake had rendered this

Fishing went bad and vast sections of the Outer Cape became a wasteland.

great fish infertile. Men of the beach, who knew no more, but certainly no less, blamed the netters in the natal rivers that feed the Chesapeake. Others said it was the coastwide combined pressure of sport fishing.

I editorialized against the bluefish, pointing out that populations of bluefish had historically been inversely proportional to those of stripers; few were prepared to argue against the fact that bluefish were everywhere. In the West Passage of Narragansett Bay, four years before, we had caught schoolies, many of them with their tail fins cut off or scarred. One surf regular, who spent some time on the Chesapeake while in the Navy, liked to tell of catching "rocks" that were scarred by predation from another species—presumably bluefish. Few of today's surfcasters remember a time when they were at normal levels. When I was a boy, fishing with my Dad in the late 40s in Narragansett Bay, a bluefish was such a rarity that people would leave good striper fishing for a chance to catch a blue. It was not until 20 years later that occasional bluefish blitzes took place.

Then there is the business of determining what level of striper population should be considered normal. Long before the influences of overfishing or pollution, the striper suffered from periodic fluctuations of abundance and scarcity. These were not what could be accurately called cycles, because there was no pattern to the amount of time that lapsed.

The greatest number of today's stripermen were born in the mid to late forties, maturing and joining the fishery during a period of heretofore unknown levels of striper abundance. They learned to expect what they had witnessed as normal levels of abundance when in fact such superabundance was never previously known, or recorded in what history was available. The perceived reduction in striper numbers may be overblown because we had just passed a 20 year period when there were more stripers available for catching. Such was the diverse picture painted by both casual and expert observers of the striped bass. But the safest explanation for loss of the species, one with widespread acceptance, was that the reason for decline was a combination of them all.

Each night we set out the way we always had, but our vitality for it often wavered. Nights when we took a fish, the adrenalin rushed through our bodies like a drug, but it nearly always ended in more failure. What rod and reel commercials we had known had gone to fluke fishing from boats in Provincetown Harbor; others went tuna fishing for the big dollars that the Japanese brought to the market. Sometimes we would meet a regular who had come out for old times and we would talk more than we ever had back when things were good. Two things dominated conversation: the bass; and, how regulations were changing in the Seashore Park.

Wood End was under renewed fire from groups of townies who had thought that the winter storms of two years before had effectively cut off access from fishermen. But the breach in the narrow barrier had been shallow enough to permit passage at low tide. Dozens of rigs crossed nightly staying around the clock until the tide permitted their escape. Traditionally, this had been both a nude and gay beach and the people who used it resented the influx of buggies, the loss of privacy. But they could not present their case for their true purposes. Rather, they objected to the vehicles on environmental grounds. Moreover, the gay community in P-Town is a formidable local force. Had environment been the real issue, the Park Service would have never permitted the hundreds of men who lived in the dune grass there to stay.

When we arrived in Provincetown ten years before, words of the District Ranger were still fresh in everyone's ears:

"Our purpose, among others, is to preserve the local culture and traditions." This was said to the fishermen of the beach. Here is how they preserved the local fishing culture:

1. They banned self-contained vehicles from Wood End.
2. Established "Self-Contained Areas" restricting those areas where they could both be driven and parked.
3. One by one they abolished those areas.
4. Fees were levied, quotas set, and days of use were counted and limited.

In all my years on the Cape, I met many people who did not care what the Park Service did to the beach buggy fishermen because they had bought the fairy lore in Cape papers about environmental degradation. What few realize is that Park management's purpose is to keep public use to a minimum because the less visitors that there are, the less problems arise. No better illustration of how the Park Service has gone out of control could be found than by having a tourist with a two-wheel-drive auto try to fish an Outer Cape beach after dark. Lovely, spacious parking lots dot the shoreline from Herring Cove to Eastham. But those, with neither the inclination nor means for a four-wheel-drive, who want to use these areas for surfcasting must have a "Fishing Permit" issued during the day at North District Headquarters. Fail to do so, and you became a contributor to the Cape's second industry—towing. Even the visitor lucky enough to know all the rules, faced a three night limitation on such permits. Understandably, the Rangers feared vandalism and carousing in the parking areas. But their solution placed all burden upon the visitor to the Park—the very person the Park Service purportedly was intent upon serving. Such guardianship, as opposed to management that served the public at large, is both proof of their insincerity and empirical evidence that beach buggying was not alone in the culpritizations of CCNS.

What a travesty it is that the finest surfcasting on the East Coast and the finest striper fishing in the world is being "preserved for our children," as goes the catchphrase, while their parents are denied out of convenience to its caretakers. Anyone could see that the days of the fishermen in the Seashore Park were limited. Everyone that we met lamented the situation, but we were all powerless to turn it around. Spoon fed in small doses, our freedoms were slipping away, always one turn of the screw, so slowly that the loss itself was barely discernible.

More easily read, more concrete in the cold, numerical facts of the accountant's ledger, were the figures for the year: Just over 2,000 pounds, all big fish, and just under $4,000. Each of us lost 15 pounds that summer, driving ourselves, determined to make it up somehow. Determined to find the bass because there had to be a hole where they could be found, we shored our spirits nightly with talk of the old days. Or I would outline conditions: Good sou'west, tide slack after sunset, nobody around. But these were mere follies from out of the past and before long we both recognized it.

CHAPTER 21

Aces and Eights

When I saw Paulie again that spring we both avoided talk of decline as though it were something of which we had both had our fill. Failing to make the connection, he talked excitedly about a leftover Bronco at the Ford dealer in town that had two grand off the sticker price. No doubt it was victim of waning interest in the beach. This was of no interest to me, so I asked him if New York's cats were safe while he indulged himself in the amenities of Cape Cod. But he paid no attention as he hugged my Joyce, reminding her that his offer still stood.

Of course his remarks about her being such a sweetheart and I so unworthy of a woman like her were never intended to be taken seriously. I took them for what I always knew he meant them to be: That I was one lucky sonofabitch to have her beside me every night. How good can it get? You marry your high school sweetheart, raise a clutch of kids, then surfcast until you die. Sounds simple, but in an age when nobody stays with anybody anymore, an age when the kids grow up his, hers, and theirs, it is a strikingly rare thing that thing that we have.

"Better head for Nauset, Nutbag," he said. "Anybody bringing in bass at the dock has to wait for the lumper to look it up in a fish book."

My failure to answer him was probably a clear signal that we planned to fish there. I grinned and told him that we would find them and he tossed his head toward one shoulder, a gesture to Joyce that he knew where we were going.

The best spot that year, 1980, was Bush Point. We caught a couple there, fish behind Long Bar an hour, then go back and stick another. We often worked the inlet to rest Bush Point; between them all, we usually could get a slow pick going. Poor nights we left Nauset early and stopped off at Balston—usually for nothing. One night we checked the Race but the sight of it all just made us sick again. Now, Wood End was closed and all the bottom fishermen had entrenched themselves at the Race because it was all they had.

It was late July, a weekend night it had to be, because there were more buggies passing us toward the inlet. Only this time nobody came back toward the north. I whistled her in and we eased the buggy through a thick fog to the inlet. Tide would flood at midnight, spring tide for the dark moon. We could have scooted the short mile with headlights on in seconds, but I preferred to slip in slowly without them; it is better for the fishing and it sets an example for the others.

Water was flying at the beach end where a gaggle of buggies had collected. I saw no fish, yet knew from the way the others were fishing that the store was open. This side of the crowd we pinned three fish with rigged eels. Oh, how I loved reaching down their throats, running my fingers along the eel's body until I got to the big siwash hook embedded in the cartilaginous roof of the mouth. I could do this without a light, without bringing attention to myself. The adrenalin was rushing through me as I felt the rush of another blitz. Tonight we would do a job, I just knew. But the casters to the left were idle now and there was still movement way right. Maybe the school had passed on its way to Pleasant Bay and would hole up in the eddy on the edge of the tip.

"Let's move," I called. Joyce stepped lively like she always does when there are fish.

Cutting sharply to the right to avoid reverse, which would have illuminated the sky with back-up lights otherwise, I nursed the buggy past the dark shadows of the rigs. Here the beach curves into a hook of sand some 400 feet wide at the base and perhaps 100 wide at the point of the hook before curving right into Pleasant Bay.

"I think we're gonna load up," I said.

And she whispered, "Looks good."

Nursing along at maybe five mile per hour, I engaged the windshield wipers, straining to keep the outlines of the other buggies in position. The idea that I was not certain exactly where we were was only a faint perception.

"If we can match what we already have two more times we're good for ...."

"FRANK!"

The buggy lurched slightly right, but still I resisted the temptation to use my brakes.

"We're in the water!"

There were no brakes, no steering.

"GET OUT!" I shouted.

"I can't!"

Jamming my shoulder against my door, I drove my body outward, but the door felt as though it were welded shut.

There were gurgling sounds all around us, amid a dozen hissing and snapping noises as the electrical system shorted.

"Get out, goddammit, get out!"

"I can't," she pleaded.

"Go out the window. I'll see you on the top."

I knew she wasn't going to make it. She would freeze there, motionless, while the sea rose around her. She has always been so sheltered from machinery, athletics, and the other things that so many of us take for granted, but which for us build skills, reaction skills—the ability to move and think under pressure. *This is going to kill her,* I thought. My mind agonizing over all the possibilities, I wanted to lead her out her window, but I could picture us both part way through.

Jesus Christ!

Hail Mary, full of grace, the Lord is with thee ...

I could see the kids kneeling at her coffin. They were all smaller. Still, the twins were in uniforms that did not fit them; Carol's party dress was too large. It was as though they had begun to go the other way. Dickie was crying and blaming me, saying that I was supposed to be taking care of Mom. It was as though we were all going to die because *she* died. It was a nightmare. I wanted it to stop. I wanted something else to happen so that I would know that this was not real.

"Oh Frank!" Her voice cracked in a raised quiver of fear. I vividly recall squeezing the release button on her seat belt, even though she was not wearing it. Less then a minute had passed, water gushing over the bottom of her window frame. There was only time for one, crisp, no-nonsense instruction:

"Go out the window! I'll see you on the top," I ordered.

Then, in the blackness, I waved my arm to the right and there was nothing. I fought the steering wheel. *I'm going to die!* I scrambled and kicked, driving my body over the window edge, while an inch of water rolled softly into the cab. Holding the door frame all the time, I then felt the buoyancy of the sea take up my weight on the outside. I stood on the hood, climbed to the roof, and found my darling waiting when I got there.

Walking among surfrods in the roof rack as if they were so much junk, we slipped out of our waders and slickers. We always leave the top of the tailgate open, but tonight, because of the dampness, I had closed it. Because of this, there was a bubble at the rear of the vehicle keeping us afloat. The silence and deadly blackness was broken only by sudden watery belches of air escaping from below. As the parking lights faded to pin lines, a vertigo sensation came over us. We not only knew nothing of where we were, but once out of the water, we couldn't even define the sky. Then came the terrifying realization that we were still lost. We were inside the hook on the end of the beach? Or, were we drifting in the currents of the inlet?

Both of us were wearing two cell, C-size flashlights. And though we probed the gray death all around us we could find no shore. Apparently we had drifted beyond the capability of these lights, or the fog overpowered them. As we stood on our sinking buggy, we wondered which way to swim. Where was land? I swung the frail light in a circle and found nothing. The only thing I could see were faint, glassy motion lines at the tailgate, clear evidence that we were drifting.

I flashed three dots and three dashes in an arbitrary direction, but realized that this was using up our time. Again I swept the light around us, this time picking up a trace of black weed that suggested sand. I could not decipher if the sand was really there or in my mind because, in the light that we had, all was gray, the moisture in the air reflecting. I tested the vision of the weed by training away from it then returning; it was there. There was momentary comfort in finding the shore, but as I sought to assess its distance, maybe 40 feet, I had the feeling we were drifting past it—perhaps, I thought, into the vicious currents of the inlet. It was a case of getting the hell out of there.

Leaving her on the roof of a sinking truck, where she might freeze, didn't seem like the right thing. What if what I thought I saw was not there? On the other hand, if she went in first and had to come back, I could be on the roof with a light to guide her. If I went in first and shore was further away then I thought, she might not find the beach and would have no way returning to the buggy ... assuming it were still afloat by then.

Laying on the roof, I couldn't touch bottom with a 9½ foot surfrod, which meant that there was some distance involved. Joyce went in first holding on to the rod for as far as she could, I thrusting her body away to pick up every free swimless inch. I could see her form working slowly away just before she called, "I'm touching." a few seconds passed—"I'm out!"

I went.

In the few minutes that passed before we found someone, we had both begun to shiver uncontrollably. "Red" Hudson, a surfman I fished with off and on with since the beginning, took us in awakening his wife, Dot, to help make us more comfortable. Word was passed to other buggies for clothes that would fit us. Joyce had a pair of men's jeans and I was wearing one of Dot's wool sweaters. God, did I love that sweater! Through the night, we sipped coffee and cognac and Joyce was never more than a foot away from me. Sometimes we talked and tried to joke about what we had done, my mind drifted.

We had been such lovers; she had been such a companion. It was a jumble of the things that we had shared in 25 years: sick kids, bills, tuition. We had cried a stream of tears through it all, but the laughter and pleasure that we had shared together in spite of it, were all things, that up to now, I had never given much thought about. Tonight, that which came so close to being our last, was an awakening to the realization of how much I loved my Joyce. There would never have been any life for me without her; and this brush with losing her brought me closer to understanding it.

Chatham police had been radioed sometime during the night and Brownie's tow truck was at the inlet a little after dawn at low tide. The buggy was upright, though tilted forward from a small prominence in the bottom which was three feet away. The regulars were all standing around, which is painful for a fellow like myself who enjoys a low profile. I tried to explain to them that we did this without headlights, that we did not want to ruin the fishing for anybody. One thoughtful observor reminded me that, "Runnin' over the bass don't help the fishin' none." I examined the used track along with a place where one set of tires went off course by 10 degrees for 100 feet before disappearing only three yards from where they should have been. However serious, my error had not been that great.

Brownie's weight was on the steel hook, keeping up the tension as the roller of the winch payed out cable. When he had enough, he looked around turning his head toward the buggy, as if wondering who owned this hulk of steel. I knew what he wanted and came forward.

Pushing the hook toward my chest, he said something about the owner-ship of the truck. I couldn't bear the thought of going back in the water. Where would the next pair of dry pants come from? Was I willing to risk the sleeves of this cozy wool sweater? The men there didn't bother me, but I knew there were a dozen wives and daughters standing around. Thus, as a final indignity from a night I already preferred to forget. I stripped down to save dry clothes, waded into not-so-Pleasant Bay just far enough to place the hook on the rear end of my buggy and annoint my own in the Atlantic amid peals of laughter that seemed to be coming from all of Cape Cod.

Within 30 hours we were driving the unwanted Bronco that Paulie had talked about. And, that fall the insurance settlement reduced the cost of moving our buggy up three years to under $2,000. It was our sense of well being that never recovered.

CHAPTER 22

Breaking Away

For both of us the sense of betrayal was overwhelming. We could no longer move about in the darkened silence that had become a trademark. Every fog, the very essence of life at night on Cape Cod, reminded us of how close we had come. Every place that we had fished, or could look longingly at from a distance, brought back memories. Somehow, something in our psyche was forcing us both to live more in the past than in the future. It was a thing that preyed upon us constantly, a burden upon our minds that intensified a sense of loss. We ended up sport fishing the salmon rivers in Maine.

For Joyce the testiness and the beauty of the fish there was meaningless. Always she questioned our reasons for hunting the rivers, the miles of casts laid end to end, for what? All sense of purpose in the challenge of salmon fishing escaped her. After a few weeks, we were back at the Cape because it was all that we could do together.

It surprised me that we were even missed by the regulars. Somehow, they knew that we had been in Maine, certain that we had located stripers there and had found a way to replace the Cape. I remember thinking that their over-speculation was born out of some inner hope that there was a frontier left. Nights working the tide rips to the east we saw no one driving the waterline trails. Yet the Race had become inundated with surfcasters. One night we drove past the lighthouse because we could neither see the water nor find room to shut down the buggy. As we approached Hatches Harbor we saw a spiked surfrod at the high water mark, unattended in the darkness, its line leading to the water. There was not another buggy within a quarter mile.

I listened for breaking fish in the currents that drifted from the estuary, casting a plug half-heartedly, when a buggy approached in parking lights and shut down. The driver reeled in the line, rebaited, cast, then drove back to the Race. Joyce was as astonished as I to see this. Never, from elbow to hook, a lifetime on the Cape, had we ever seen anyone spread a series of set rods over an area so large. But the deed was merely a reflection of the desperation that had come to surfcasters there. For us it was going out each night to quit an hour earlier or listen to 'oldies music' on the radio. For him, whoever he was, a surfrod that was driving distance away, but alone on that particular shore, represented some small hope for a striped bass.

Another night we met Paulie whom we had not seen since the buggy sinking. He was particularly warm, hugging my Joyce first before he talked to me, asking about the girls and as to why she would stick it out with a graying old man who was losing it fast, who also made a habit of buying up other people's toys. I savored his every word.

"Frank, they are killing us. Two more years and there will be nothing left. Look at the Race, enough to make you sick. They're getting ready to close the whole back beach clear to Eastham. Vince wants to form a coalition, take names, have newsletters, show up at meetings, find a way to fight these bastards."

I could tell by the way that Paulie was talking that he wanted me to do something. That was a thing about many of the surfmen: They believed that a writer could turn anything around just by writing about it. But fishing writers talk to fishermen. Besides, what would we be fighting to save a

When the bassfishing went downhill we tried salmon fishing in Maine but it just wasn't the same.

beach for with stripers gone?

I covered the funeral of the outer Cape for *The New England Fisherman* in the way that a detached reporter might. I tried to report the facts about losing the finest 35 miles of striper surf in the world. The North District Ranger told me that they had edicts from three different Presidents requiring control of recreational vehicles in National Parks. It seemed to matter to no one that the meaning and intent of these orders was with inland parks in mind. The basis of concern had been born out of small ATV's that tore up the vegetation in places like Yosemite and Yellowstone, not seashore parks, which have unique environmental concerns. But instead I was in attendance at the burial of a friend. The North District Ranger knew what the intent of those Presidential edicts had been. And each lie was just another shovelful of earth upon the grave of a Cape Cod that we had so come to love.

Our last year in P-Town we were mere visitors after a string of poor nights at Nauset. After the usual *post mortem* visit to the Race, we struck east again toward the Mission Bell. Near the Traps I noticed headlights in the trail behind us and responded to my suspicion by dropping my speed. It slowed. We stopped to fish. It stopped. We hid among the buggies of Race City. A ranger vehicle passed. Later, near the Mission Bell, a set of headlights came out of nowhere when we moved. I don't know how many rangers were involved in this cat and mouse game, but we were followed three times, really never alone those few hours on the beach.

Joyce must have sensed my irritation when I stopped the buggy, waving the ranger on to inquire about his purpose.

"Frank," she pleaded, "Not now, we have everything!"

Gritting my teeth, I was hoping that he would make one more mistake; that he might give me an excuse to raise the price. As I approached the patrol vehicle, he turned on the blue strobe, a device more often used as a tool of intimidation than the announcement of any emergency. I allowed him to speak first:

"Good evening, Sir, do you have a problem Sir?"

There is a salt-upon-the-wound feeling that comes from being "sirred" too many times. Here, a middle aged couple is surfcasting on the beach in a legal area with a beach permit and there are more armed gestapo than surfcasters. Arrogance aside, there was something in his voice, a youthful harmlessness that broke down my urge for aggression. It isn't that I had lost my nerve; rather, I had regained my senses. What point was there in trying to bring him out? He was, after all, an instrument of policy and if I dared try to vent my irritation with him I would lose in the end. Keeping my voice low, I asked why he and other rangers were following us; what violation did they hope to catch us at?

I walked back to the buggy during his response and never visited the Provincelands again. At another time in my life it might have gone differently. But we had everything. The children were gone, the two mortgages were paid off, most of the fish money had doubled. We were both established professionals. Was I fool enough to throw it all away on some dark night for a man that symbolized our overwhelming sense of frustration?

How many times can you cut your annual catch by half before it becomes nothing? By 1984 the legal minimum size had been raised to 24 inches to protect a few consecutive year-classes of schoolies that had begun to bang and swat our plugs. With them we might have made it as commercials, but with striper fishing what it was, sentiments what they were, it was best that they be left alone.

By then the Atlantic States Marine Fisheries Commission (ASMFC) was

By 1984 the legal minimum size had been raised to 24 inches to protect a few consecutive year classes that had begun to hit our lures.

trying to iron out management policy that the striper states could live with. Commercial fishermen, netters, were fighting it on the grounds that sport fishermen were making no concessions. The feeling among ASMFC officials was that all high harvest activity had to be stopped. Early hopes had been pinned upon the Chesapeake's '78 year class but it was ravaged, reportedly by Chesapeake watermen. Subsequently, commercial activity stopped there, the last holdouts were haul seiners on Long Island and fish traps in Rhode Island. By the time the '82 year class was large enough to migrate, all the netting had stopped and there were enough stripers around, dangerously close to legal size, for size limits to be raised to 30 inches for sport fishermen. Moreover, daily limits fell into place in many striper states to prevent the inevitable waste that so often comes in saltwater fishing.

I don't know why a no-sell law was never tried again. By the early 80's the time was right for it, the situation far different from when it had failed over 10 years before. Certainly, opposition to a no-sell law would have been minimal. Instead a strange quirk of striper biology came to the species's rescue—PCB's.

All during the period of heavy striper marketing, many of the fish—those from the Hudson—contained levels of PCB's. But these were within the allowable limits of 5 parts per million (ppm). Then the food and drug administration reduced the allowable tolerance level for PCB's in food fish to 2 ppm. Around that time Rhode Island found that 93% of the stripers over 24 inches they tested failed the new FDA limit. There, officials claimed that they had one fish with levels so high that it qualified as "hazardous waste." Other Hudson River averages tested as high as 3.9 ppm. That year Massachusetts tested stripers from 12 to 42 pounds, a size that would yield greater concentrations, finding an average PCB level of 1.1 ppm; only one fish exceeded standards at 2.11. Because Hudson River stripers largely failed to meet these standards for contamination, New York state banned the sale of the species. The effect of this was closure of the largest fish market in the world—Fulton Street—to the sale of striped bass.

Reduction in the allowable level of PCB contamination generated de facto no-sell protection for bass nearly coastwide. Without Fulton Street, bass prices fell from $3.00 per pound to under a dollar, dramatically reducing incentives in what few places, like Massachusetts, where commercial fishing could continue. Of course there has been no netting allowed for stripers in the Bay State for decades. Indeed, PCB's turned out to be the friend of striped bass, particularly when we take into account that the contaminant has no apparent effect upon the species's overall pathology.

The curious melange of regulations intended to protect the Chesapeake's '82 year class, and the PCB concerns that render Hudson River stripers unmarketable cross shelter the two populations. There is no way of knowing which race of lineside is in the hand—the one too valuable to eat, or the one too poisonous. It was either a joyous accident of conversation or a brilliant strike of backroom planning on the part of somebody that the two have attained protection.

The curious melange of regulations intended to protect the Chesapeake's '82 year class and the PCB concerns that rendered Hudson River stripers unmarketable cross-sheltered the two populations.

CHAPTER 23

Striper Comeback

Chesapeake Bay has customarily been the major source of *Morone saxatilis* stocks from New Jersey to the Canadian Maritimes. Research conducted by Texas Instruments for ConEd of New York determined that over 90% of the bass taken in mid-Atlantic coastal waters in 1974 were of Chesapeake origin. Thus, any examination of striper decline calls for close scrutiny of the condition of the nation's largest estuary. Labeled as "an ecosystem in decline" by the EPA, the Chesapeake is on the edge of losing an annual 750 million dollar seafood industry. Along with the conspicuous absence of bass, other elements of the food chain—oysters, clams, and varieties of baitfish and flora—are either missing or radically reduced. Tributary rivers where stripers spawn carry sewerage, nitrogen, phosphorus, and metals to what the EPA termed the world's largest septic tank—the Chesapeake. Moreover, research completed in 1985 on the Choptank and Nanticoke Rivers—major striper nurseries—revealed a strong link between acid rain episodes and the decline of river bass populations.

While viability, the striper's ability to reproduce, was the most suspect cause of decline, the fish had been hounded from its birthplace to the coast of Maine by both commercial and sport fishing interests. The combined commercial take, comprised largely of fish from 12 to 18 inches, between the years 1954 and 1981 from the states of Maryland, Virginia and North Carolina alone was over 71% of the total commercial bass fishing activity for the entire 12 striper states on the East Coast. The sport fishing harvest, lacking the detailed measurement of commercially traded fish, was often thought to be as great.

However, with commercial moratoriums in the south and suspended netting in both New York and Rhode Island, the striper slaughters no longer occur. Sport fishing regulations which allow bag limits between zero and two fish, in tight seasons, with length limits that grew each year, always ahead of and larger than the bulk of reemerging populations, have prevented the cumulative harvest that would have probably been as great as that of netting. One would think that all this protection was too little too late were it not for reports from all over the Striper Coast of fantastic numbers of linesides.

From Montauk to Plum Island fishing reports bristled with news of school bass, their size and numbers growing each season from 1984 on. Where did they come from?

Spawning success on the Hudson River, formerly the second rate, 10% contributer of our striper stocks, enjoyed incomparable success. John Waldman, staff biologist for the Hudson River Foundation, reported unusually high juvenile indices for the years '82, '83, '84 and near or above average reproduction seven of the nine years prior to '86. Name a traditional hot spot for striped bass and you will find them there. The only remaining mystery lies in determining which race—Chesapeake or Hudson—they are from.

To my knowledge, little or no research has ever been done to sample coastwide what part of the burgeoning population is of a particular race. This could be done by measurement of PCB levels. However, if what we've been told of the Chesapeake is true, then we must surmise that the striper

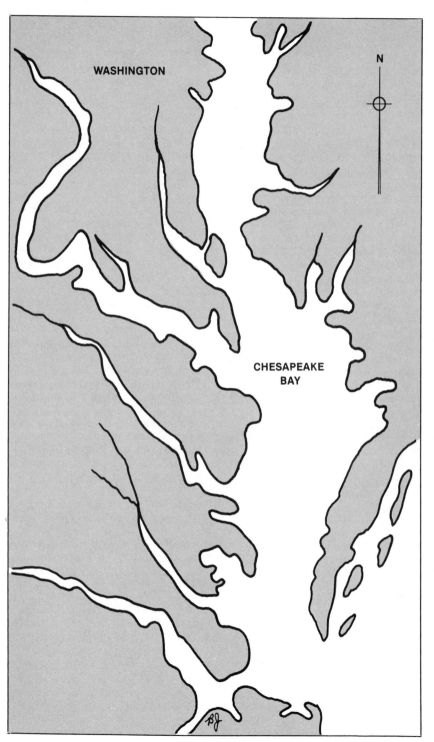

recovery in our fore is from the Hudson. This brings us to the subject of measurement, striper management, government, conservation, and ethic.

You will recall that in my life on Cape Cod I was repeatedly a victim of a system of duplicity, where there was often a secret intent for some arbitrary regulation. Sections of the beach were closed to protect birds; other places were out-of-bounds to prevent erosion when in fact it was local cottage owners who simply wanted more privacy. Wood End was closed to beach-buggies because of environmental degradation when in fact a special interest user group wanted a beach where they could be free from the exhaust of motor vehicles. In some cases, scientific studies were used to support a position, as with driving over buried shellfish, to produce a well orchestrated outcome. Officials financed, and no doubt influenced, the conclusions of science. In my mind I have come to believe that environmental protection, management and science are being steered, results being altered, in the name of a particular mission that those responsible deem of greater importance. Such a lack of managerial integrity—a snail darter mentality with a greater mission in mind—is a threat to the future of both wildlife and wild land management.

Certainly such a situation causes me to question the motives of fisheries managers and the wisdom of their means of bringing such management about. I understand that the striped bass must be saved. But there have to be things, in the everyday dealings and negotiations of managers with managers, people with people, that are even more important than striped bass: to name just one, reputability. What are we to believe?

Late in 1986 the National Oceanic and Atmospheric Administration told the Congress that seafood customers who procure bluefish were not at risk because the species represented only a portion of their seafood consumption. The study of 4,258 bluefish of all sizes between Massachusetts and Florida, from January to November of 1985, showed up to 45 percent of the fish at each sampling site *exceeded* the 2 ppm action level. It is reasonable to say that there is no public health risk with bluefish when there is with striped bass? Both exceed tolerance levels of PCB's.

In our desperation to save marine species are we willing to undermine public confidence? Does not the trade off become a threat to all future efforts, through its lack of integrity, when, down the line we will be fighting to save tuna or some other fish? Might those we seek meaningful negotiations with remember? Yes, I applaud some of what has been done, is being done, to save the striped bass. I marvel at its success. But the mission of striper preservation should have been strong enough to stand on its own merits. It should not have been saved through a numbers game where tolerable levels of PCB's were changed to render the species unmarketable. If taking bass off the market was necessary, and it was, than a no-sell law for conservation reasons was the only true course of action. Of less importance, but still worthy of mention, is that public health warnings will become meaningless if our agencies so charged are ever suspected of involving themselves in fisheries preservation.

This lack of veracity is responsible—in the largest part—for all the stripers in our surf today. And you, dear patient, loyal, readers, when you try to fish at the Cape Cod National Seashore and other parks on a growing list, are victims of the very same cunning. Management, such as that enumerated above, may have saved your striped bass, but it also closed your beaches.

In our 20 years on Cape Cod we witnessed heavier regulation of beaches which was directly attributable to increased use brought about by better

We were told bluefish were contaminated the PCB's. What were the true concerns, public health or politics?

fishing. The Park Service told me, every time a closure took place, that the numbers of oversand vehicles registered there had increased and they had. Yet, the most significant loss, the 30 miles from High Head to Eastham, took place in the fall of '85 after striper populations, and beach use, plummeted. With 90 percent of the beach closed to oversand vehicles, inaccessible by any other means, virtually gated shut during the night-time hours when the only viable surfcasting can take place, surfcasters have in effect been banished. Even that small section where vehicles are allowed from Race Light east is so compressed, overcrowded by vehicles that formerly were disbursed, that the quality of recreation there is seriously wanting, to say nothing of the police state atmosphere.

When I am told by a wildlife professional that a species is endangered, I want to know that the basis for his saying so comes from truthful analysis of the situation. When I am told by government land managers that the environment is at risk because of some misuse by the public at large, I want to be able to believe what he says. In both cases—wildlife or environment—these are professionals who are both trained for the mission and entrusted with carrying it out. We save striped bass by manipulating the allowable levels of poisons in their flesh; we satisfy the selfish desires of local citizen advisory groups on environmental grounds. This is not management of wildlife and their environment, these are lies. We can't have people that no one can believe doing these jobs. What will happen later when they come forward with the truth when grappling with some other issue?

Indeed, the Atlantic striper populations on the verge of exploding, the loss of Outer Cape Cod becomes all the more dramatic. It is here that the people of New York, New Jersey, Connecticut, who are denied access to the beach at home, want to come. It is here that striper advocacy is rewarded. Instead, local jurisdictions elsewhere harass anglers at the behest of local residents who seek control of a shore far beyond the limits of their own property. In other words, you can't go anywhere. Having a National Park to fish from once was the only hope and that has turned out to be tantamount to having the fox guard the chickens. For all that has been done to save the striped bass, virtually nothing is being done to assure access to that striped bass. We have spoken so much of striper fishing past, but access should be our greatest concern for the future.

My 20 years on Cape Cod was then, and this is now.

The Chatham Inlet we had come to love. Would it ever be the same?

CHAPTER 24

Holy Place

It was as though the cast of characters of our play of life were deserting the set and the workmen were carting off the props, and I was pleading for everyone to stop.

Enough years had passed that we knew that Dickie might come home. He had finished his enlistment earlier, but stayed on the Alaskan coast working in canneries to support his hunting and fishing. Mom and I had just gotten back from Quebec salmon fishing when this tall bearded sourdough came through the door to put us both in tears. After settling in, he talked of fishing in Alaska, silvers teeming in the estuaries, bears a thousand pounds feeding in the pools. Then he would ask about the beach, or reminisce about some time when the fishing had been good, stirring associations in the memory.

It was that way when we got back to the beach. The kid tooled the short four-by gently along the waterline trail, the headlights seeming to cause the gray mist on the horizon to dance with each gentle roll in the beach sand. It was a slow track more because Dickie, now in his mid-twenties, seemed to want to savor the feel of the machine, lengthen the anticipation of the coming tide. He chattered incessantly:

"We can check the inlet but if they are not there we can do the Scup Hole then come back. By then Long Bar will be down enough for us to try the channel, don't you think? Maybe drop down to the Refigerator Hole by daybreak, run low beach off."

It was a strange feeling to have him at the wheel. Like part of me was there, driving, yet another part of me was victim to the multi-layered sensation that the shore always renders while slowing the insistent thrust of time. Among the dunes nothing seems to have changed, except a tight place across from Chatham Light where the beach has retreated closer to Pleasant Bay. I try to decipher the stark similarity of the seascape as unchanged as the boy who leads me back to the place as though I had never known it. The closer we get the more I wonder who I am, the younger one beside me, assuring me that we will soon be there, or the one sitting beside him. I imagined the little girls playing in the sand with their pails; then taller, more feminine silhouettes of them backing from the waterline with bowed rods. A hundred scenes from a thousand nights scrolled past my mind too quickly to savor, yet stopping arbitrarily out of sheer, desperate force—one time on Susan's stationery:

"Dear Mom and Dad,

......Today we arrived in Boston for "Tall Ships". It was a sight I will always remember seeing the thousands of people with all the colors of their clothes looking like an ever-so-large patch of flowers. But most of all it was what I felt when we took in sail off Chatham to pick up an older-than-your-grandfather admiral. From the mast I could see the buggies at the inlet. And though it was not there, I could see our buggy and you, Dad, were smoking your pipe while Mom was reading. The same thing, the same sight, came to me later when we rounded Race Point. I felt so lonely and wanted to tell other cadets what I was feeling but they could never know, never understand, which is why I have to

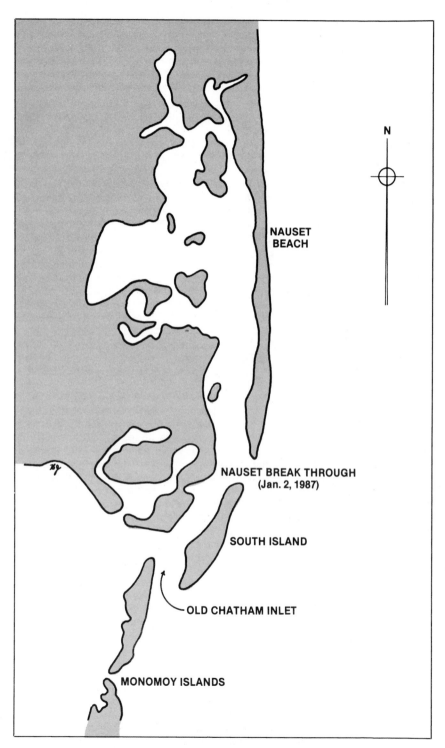

N

NAUSET
BEACH

NAUSET BREAK THROUGH
(Jan. 2, 1987)

SOUTH ISLAND

OLD CHATHAM INLET

MONOMOY ISLANDS

South Island across the new Chatham cut which is nearly a mile wide, choking off access to the old Chatham Inlet.

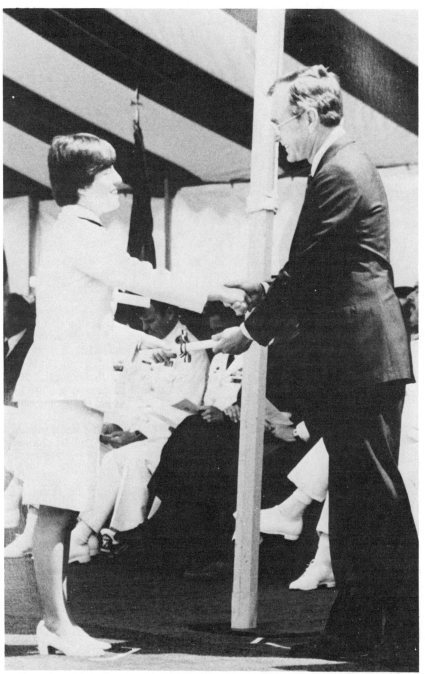

Our daughter Susan receiving her commission at the Coast Guard Academy from then Vice President George Bush.

write to you guys.

I had duty the first day playing tour guide for the visitors to the *Eagle*. Then we went ashore to 'splice up the main'."......

Love,
Susan

"Where went the bush at Bush Point?" Dick chided, while slapping me good naturedly on the shoulder, as we moved along in parking lights behind Long Bar, rousing me from thoughts of when we were simple enough to be good.

Dick's manic run to the sea as we arrived was to me a fitting acknowledgement that Alaska had failed to change him; perhaps the others were safe. Dropping the tailgate to sit, I tried to seem casual, outwardly benign, because I knew what he could not know. First, he ran a few steps then swung the rod with a swish sending the plug out over the current. There was a pause while line straightened, then the rod arced as he called, "Over here!" I did go over *sans* rod.

"Dad, get your rod," he whispered. "We'll do a job."

The lineside that scurried down the wash would have been 16 to the box in the old days. Now it represented a chance for me to tell him what had happened to the good life. We sat together on the tailgate. Trying to sound sympathetic, I explained that no one knew why but the bass of the Chesapeake were not giving up successful year classes any more. That to us there seemed to be as many fish as ever.

We are together again, alone because Mom knows that this is a special pilgrimage that we must make together. His graying mentor, who in the darkest night sees his mother's eyes in his, is beside him. Together we cast eel flies with shooting heads, the single hooks penetrating their mark with ease. Each fish fights for its life for it does not know of the vicarious death game we play. It might fear the final thud of a billy but now we are only players who do not tell until the last moment....when the point slides backward, that it is only a game.

And each time one of us yields a little more fly line, or a greater measure of backing, the other inquires of the size. Once, after Dickie chases a lineside around a distant bend in the beach, I ask him how big it was. And he, acknowledging days past, and as his way of telling me that he at long last understands, casually replies, "About six bucks."

Two years, maybe three, pass with a sameness that is routine for others. But everything that we do is doomed to failure because of the test of comparisons that haunts us no matter how far we go from Cape Cod. There is no cleansing the squid stink and salt spray from our souls. Winters, we are thankful, are the same. Some years the twins come from distant duty stations or Carol visits with her two babies; Dickie is never far away. Whenever we are together someone always talks of a time at the shore and I must face a window to hide the tears that well up of when the world was young.

January 2, 1987. The massive low pressure area traveled slowly out of the sou'west packing 60 knot winds and depositing deep snow as it went. The Petty Officer at Chatham Station listened to advisories having given up looking outside because visibility was less than 300 feet. Snow swirled and wafted in sheets across Pleasant Bay while small whitecaps developed against the shore.

On the barrier beach the vibrations of falling walls of water pound their sibilance upon the sand relentlessly. As the tide rises the lower places of Nauset Beach yield rivulets of sea that rush for the back yet dissipate before they can muster any movement in the sand. It is a battle between the permanence of time and the forces of the night. The beach seems to shore itself against that which it has known before, but it is weakened, stretched too thin, overextended. Each powerful comber pounding the shore faces a weaker adversary as clumps of dune grass bend away from the nor'east. Some fall amid the foam, others have their roots exposed as more of the water survives the absorbancy of the beach. Like the weakness in a defending fortress, the sea seems to know where it can find passage sending streams of foaming water that carries more sand to the bay. Weakness begets weakness and strength intensifies as shoal upon shoal batters the dying beach, ripping sand stored over the centuries while a thousand tons breach and rush until all sand, it seems, is in retreat.

Within minutes, the work of a hundred bulldozers is done by a North Atlantic that is amuck with rage, mindless of the tedious, pebble by pebble knitting of time. Near Scup Hole, there is a silence as all resistance is swept inland and the sea marches freely through the opening, victorious in the destruction of Nauset Beach.

By summer the breach is over a half mile wide, cast in the green hue of depth. But the Chatham Inlet we had known is starved for current, because the tides have found a better way. On what is now South Island, a scraggly bush decays amid the sands at the holy place we had once loved. Few will ever again cast the Chatham Inlet we had known. The sweet wind, having labored the centuries to build the beach, betrayed us in one night.

CHAPTER 25

Cape Cod Today

We had a life on Cape Cod, but we don't have it anymore. Some weeks we pick a quiet night when the tides are favorable to fish the new inlet. There are more bass than we have ever seen, though they are wanting in size what with size limits at 33 inches. We cast flies with our salmon rods, then let them go. But the old habits and feeling die hard.

Now we pay the price for the life we had because there is some deeply ingrained value structure in the mind that has irreversably corrupted us; we are slaves of the market price without a market. Time was when we were spurred on until the next dawn by the promise of riches. In spite of yearning for sleep, or an aching body, we drove ourselves because the fish money was the solution to our eternal curse. It was such a perfect economic system, unfettered by nepotism, featherbedding, stewards, or crony management. In effect, commercial fishing was the essence of a free economy, a model of a natural socioeconomic system the way it was once meant to be. If the fishing was good, it was easy—and the price of fish was low. On the other hand, times when nobody could find them, there were handsome rewards for those with the wit and stamina to locate and harvest. It is almost laughable that today's innovative managers speak of incentives when they want to boost production; maybe they onced fished for money.

But I was going to say that we were never able to go back to the attitudes we had before meeting Muff, when we fished for the fun of it. It was not he that corrupted us really, rather, my love and I were victims of both the search for adventure and our low economic status. Having a broker and being loaded with family money deprives you of the kind of excitement that we shared. There has to be some compensation for being born poor, marrying and making yourself poorer. Pity that I did not know at the time how filthy rich we really were. On the other hand, did we fail to seize the day?

To some degree there are others who feel a similar loss. But if the intensity of that loss relates directly to how many years were spent full-time fishing commercially on the Cape's beaches then they can take comfort in less suffering. We were first in and last out. We, after all never even considered taking to the boats because we were a family first. Moreover, we were surf casters and could never have acknowledged defeat so openly.

In any analysis of Cape Cod today one feels compelled to envy those who fish its beaches with any vitality. They are a new generation who are spared comparisons of what it once was. Many drive a few hours from inland, as we did; others seek to escape the locked up shores and tow-trucks of their home states. For them, just standing on the sand a few hours in the moonlight is an exhilirating experience. But, sadly, they are as doomed as we were.

In the spring of '88 the U.S. Fish and Wildlife Service (F&WS) initiated regulations for the protection of the piping plover on Monomoy Island. Among other things, there is a prohibition of night fishing at specific sites during the nesting season, all of which is during the time when people might be fishing for striped bass. At this writing the F&WS is going to increase staff for the writing of permits for access to Monomoy. Purportedly, the permits will guarantee that visitors will go there more informed about closed areas, regulations, and "lesson environmental impacts". All the while boundless, fantastic quantities of gulls ravage the nests of all shorebirds there. The situation here is so mindful of when they forbade surf-casters to use two miles of Provincelands beach if they were a threat to one endangered tern....while a fox ate them nightly!

But there is a certain irony in issuing permits to surfcasters who risk the dangerous crossing by boat nightly. It is these very men whose cars were towed from parking lots at Lecount, Newcomb Hollow, and Race Point. They started crossing to Monomoy to escape the frivolous regulation of CCNS; they found it easier to cross by boat once than drive 20 miles to the Park for a permit during the day and then return there at night.

Dr. William Muller, a fisherman and writer who is intimate with the situation in the coastal mid-Atlantic says, "Closing down the beaches has reached epidemic proportions resulting in the loss of access to law-abiding people. It is convenience rather than logic."

We saw both the striped bass and access to the beaches decline. But only the striped bass is coming back. As a society we may have better skills in the restoration of species than in managing habitat to the satisfaction of the majority. I'm thankful that the life held up long enough for the kids to grow out of it, that they were spared the anguish of watching the pieces of it cast adrift. How do you come back from that kind of life?

Still, we search for the magic. The dogs point smartly in frosty New England meadows and Joyce moves in for a shot. Later, around the first snow, we cut saplings beside prominent bucks. Summers we shoot clay targets, hearing the scorer call "loss" more times than we would like. Or, we pay the Ministry $100 per day to cast in salmonless rivers. Each endeavor reminds us how painful it is to do something badly; our life on Cape Cod conditioned us to feel good about ourselves. It was so delicious to be the best in the business. It is so degrading now to be among the worst; occasionally, there are some moments when the magic makes its momentary pass and we rise to mediocrity.

At the gun club *le haute monde* shudder at each rain drop, each wind gust that dares assault their attire. The salmon are neat what with their jumps and pugnacity. And the salmon pools are visited by polite gentlemen who boast of their insanity as though they were the only ones who had cornered the market on self-imposed misery. I smile politely, pretending to be one of them, but inside—I dare not say—they are so effete, such pansies. No matter how rainy it can get on a salmon river, it never gets as dark as a closet. Riffles don't pull in the same way as tide rips; nor do rivers get as pushy as Cape Cod surf.

Summer 1988. One of the casters called to us:

"Hey Buddy, fish are all over the place!"

He pointed to his rod arcing, breaking my thought pattern, my Joyce pretending not to see him. And I tried to forget that no matter where I look I cannot find that fleeting thing, that inscrutable drama, that we once had known.

The striper is coming back but for those of us who knew it when it was good the Cape can never be the same.

About The Author

Frank Daignault published his first article on surf fishing in *Salt Water Sportsman* magazine in 1970. Since then his hundreds of articles have appeared in *Fishing World, Sports Afield, Outdoor Life, Fins and Feathers, Salmon Trout and Steelheader, Fly Fishing, The Fisherman Papers, Gun World* and *Shotgun Sports.* Among his hardcover contributions are sections in *Peterson's Complete Book of Sportfishing, Mariner's Catalog, Surf Fishing With The Experts* and *All About Surf Fishing.* He has been a columnist for *Striper Magazine* since 1978.

Daignault has lectured on striped bass and surfcasting for outdoor exhibitions and fishing clubs around New England since 1979. As a member of the New England Outdoor Writers Association, he was honored in 1983 by the Daiwa Corporation for his encouragement of youth fishing. He is also a member of the Outdoor Writers of America. A teacher in Johnston, Rhode Island, he holds a Masters Degree in Industrial Education.